George Harrison ॐ +

the dark horse years 1976 – 1992

Artwork Design:
thenewno2 with Drew Lorimer (redroom@emi)

Illustration:
Page 24 – Ganesh page design by Jan Steward

Photographs:
Cover Photo – © Terry O'Neill
Page 6 – George with guitar; pages 7, 9, 12, 16 & 17 – © Terry O'Neill
Page 6 – George with Jerry Moss – © Christian Rose
Page 6 – George with Mo Ostin – courtesy of Warner Bros.
Pages 19, 22 & 23 – "When We Was Fab" – Photographer Unknown
Page 19 – George & Olivia at Midem, 1977 – © Michael Putland
Page 21 – © Peter Figen
Additional Photography: © thenewno2

ISBN 0-634-09559-5

7777 W. Bluemound Rd. P.O. Box 13819 Milwaukee, WI 53213

Visit Hal Leonard Online at
www.halleonard.com

contents

the history of dark horse 1976 – 1992

The *year* 1976 *marked the end of* George Harrison's *recording contract with* EMI/Parlophone. It *was first negotiated for the* Beatles *as a group by* Brian Epstein *in* 1962 *and renewed in* 1967 *with additional rights as solo artists.*

Over a span of fourteen years, thirteen original Beatle albums, several compilations and six solo albums were released. George looked forward to a change with such anticipation that in 1974 he created his own label. Although it would be two years before his contractual obligations were fulfilled, Dark Horse Records was ready for George's arrival.

The Dark Horse label was distributed initially by Herb Alpert and Jerry Moss's A&M Records, situated at the old Charlie Chaplin Studios on La Brea Avenue in Hollywood. In October 1974, I was there to welcome George to his new office. We shared the ground floor of a two-storey bungalow with Lou Adler's Ode Records. Having worked at A&M for the previous two years I knew how

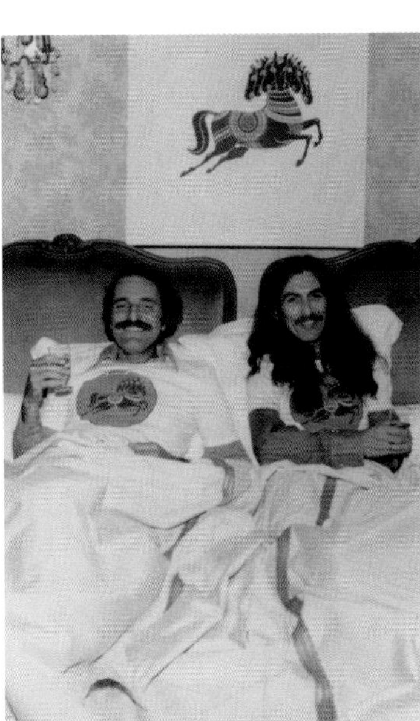

George with A&M Owner Jerry Moss

George with Warner Bros. President Mo Ostin and his button

DARK HORSE

much prestige George would bring to any record company. Not only had he been in the Beatles, but after the break-up of the band, George's first solo album, *All Things Must Pass*, reached number one. The *Concert for Bangladesh* and *Living in the Material World* were still fresh in our minds and George was held in high esteem by us all.

George spent a good deal of time at the Dark Horse office while recording his own album, *Extra Texture*, in A&M studios. Over two years, eight albums were released by artists on his label. Ravi Shankar, the band Attitudes (with friend Jim Keltner), the duo Splinter from Sheffield (produced by George), R&B vocal group The Stairsteps, ex-Joe Cocker guitarist Henry McCullough and a California band named Jiva made up the Dark Horse roster.

By the time George came to release *Thirty Three & 1/3* — his first album for the label, Dark Horse had moved to Warner Bros. in Burbank.

A Birth Announcement.

Mo Ostin had stepped in to sign George for what would be the remainder of his solo music career, as well as two albums with *The Traveling Wilburys*. George enjoyed the Warner family, even recruiting Warner Bros. staff for the video of 'This Song' from *Thirty Three & 1/3* and he remained close friends with Mo Ostin for the rest of his life.

George recorded six Dark Horse albums from 1976 to 1992. They contained songs written while he was in the Beatles including, 'See Yourself' and 'Not Guilty' right up to 'Cheer Down,' written at the request of Dick Donner, the director of *Lethal Weapon* 2.

Some of George's songs were featured in movies made by his company Handmade Films, including, 'Shanghai Surprise' from the much-talked-about but little-seen Sean Penn and Madonna movie and 'Dream Away' from Terry Gilliam's *Time Bandits*.

Listening to the albums in chronological order, George's evolution as a songwriter, guitarist and seeker are obvious. 'Mystical One' and 'Your Love Is Forever' are my favourite ballads; the type of love song Eric Clapton describes as spiritual love songs. In fact, George wrote 'Mystical One' with Eric ('shimmering slowhand') in mind. 'Devil's Radio' was his comment on gossip and 'Life Itself,' 'Circles' and 'Dear One' clear expressions of his spirituality. He wrote for himself as well as others but without premeditation for commercial success. Some of these albums received more acclaim than others. The reward was in the creation of his songs as well as the companionship of other musicians during the recording

Statistics

sessions. All George's creativity, attention and unexpressed emotion went into his music. Once an album was delivered, the least enjoyable part for him (promotion and press) would commence. Sometimes he cooperated wholeheartedly, sometimes not. Whatever the outcome, he did not wait around for approval before beginning the writing process over again.

The Dark Horse has come full circle now— back with EMI/Parlophone since 2002— and the seven-headed horse still spins George's name and music according to his own plan. George chose this symbol to be at the forefront of his musical legacy— a legacy now firmly imprinted in this material world and the spiritual sky beyond.

Olivia Harrison
November 2003
Oxfordshire, England

The Dark Horse Logo

On one of George's many visits to India, the drawing of a seven-headed horse on the side of a tin box caught his eye. Always one to appreciate a mystical symbol, he carried the small tin back to England and adapted it as the logo for Dark Horse Records.

Known as Uchchaisravas, the seven-headed horse appears often in Indian art and mythology (the Puranas).
His story of origin tells of a time when there were so many demons threatening the world that the gods had become weak. Lord Vishnu whipped up a tonic—an elixir of immortality—by churning the Ocean of Beginnings.
Uchchaisravas, the seven-headed horse appeared from the milky sea as did the goddess Laxmi and

many other creatures. In some stories the enchanted horse pulls the chariot of Krishna and his disciple, Arjuna. Sometimes he is seen hitched to the chariot of the sun god, Surya or the mount of the god Indra.

In the West, of course, we often refer to a person with hidden talents as a dark horse, a thought for which George had an affinity. It was not unusual for George to express himself with symbology that contained both Eastern and Western connotations. 'Create and preserve the image of your choice,' said Mahatma Ghandi. It was a quote George used frequently, and his choice of this horse was as deliberate as any other image he associated with his music or himself.

george harrison dark horse

At the top of the original inner sleeve for George Harrison's 1981 album, *Somewhere in England*, were the words of Sri Krishna in the *Bhagavad-Gita*: 'There was never a time when I did not exist, nor you. Nor will there be any future when we cease to be.' It was a dedication from Harrison to his friend and fellow Beatle, John Lennon.

Those words are a lesson and a comfort; a reassurance from Harrison himself that he is very present in the world. Particularly on the records in this collection.

Harrison's entire life in music was a search for a balanced inner peace; a reconciliation of the earthly rewards of rock 'n' roll with a higher lasting wisdom. These six albums were a big part of that life, and our knowledge of him is incomplete without them. This wonderful library of warm soulful singing, bright incisive guitar playing, secular lyrical mischief and serene prayer is long overdue for rediscovery – and, more importantly, sharing. 'It only takes time 'til love comes to everyone,' Harrison sang over the church-bell strum and beatific stroll of 'Love Comes to Everyone.' The time has come.

Remember that Harrison was only 26 in 1970, when the Beatles broke up and he astonished the mourners with his triumphant, sumptuous solo debut, *All Things Must Pass*.

Then consider this: He was just 33 when he started making this music for his own label, Dark Horse. Over the next 16 years he produced films, became an avid gardener, entered fatherhood, grieved for Lennon, collaborated with friends and mentors such as Eric Clapton, Bob Dylan and Ravi Shankar and, one last time, went on tour. Harrison's middle age was a rich, busy, creatively vital period, and he put it all in song, playing some of the finest guitar of his career and singing with relaxed assurance. The spaces between albums got longer, but Harrison was no longer a 'Solo Artist' in the self-promoting, music-biz sense. He was simply a Musician again.

'George was a reluctant rock star, but he loved to play rock 'n' roll,' says Jeff Lynne. He first met Harrison in the mid-Eighties when asked to co-produce *Cloud Nine*, and remained a close friend for the rest of Harrison's life. 'At the end of a session,' Lynne continues, 'around two in the morning, we'd have a few drinks, listen back to the stuff we'd been doing and then start playing other songs together, some of his old favorites. He didn't like the bullshit that goes with being famous. But he loved to make music, and he loved recording. He really liked making demos – getting songs down fast, then leaving them alone.'

'Guitars, basic drums and analog tape – that's the way I like it,' Harrison confirmed years later in *Rolling Stone*. 'It doesn't go with trends. My trousers don't get wider and tighter every six months. My music just stays what it is, and that's it.' That's what you hear on these records: Harrison at his most honest and musically pure, playing what he wanted to hear, the way he liked to hear it, when the time was right.

Harrison Signs with Dark

■ CANNES, FRANCE — George Harrison and Dark Horse Records have jointly announced that Harrison has signed a multiple record agreement with the company, effective January 27, 1976. A first Harrison album for the label is scheduled for late spring or early summer release.

In conversation with **Record World,** Harrison exuded new energy, approaching the Dark Horse agreement as a challenge akin to that of the early Beatles career. At the official announcement, Harrison said, "I feel very optimistic being in the company of the Dark Horse artists and staff, and greatly encouraged by my past relationship with Herb (Alpert), Jerry (Moss) and the staff of A&M."

Production Plans

In addition, Harrison stated that he was thinking of using an outside producer in order to free himself for artistic considerations. The former Beatle began his songwriting career in November 1963 with "Don't Bother Me." He contributed over the years to the various Beatle albums and films

I met Harrison at one of those times, in November 1976 at a press-the-flesh affair in Washington, D.C. to celebrate the release of *Thirty-Three & 1/3*. He shook my hand warmly, autographed a promotional photo and flashed an enigmatic smile with me for my friend's camera. It was a remarkable moment for me and it changed the way I listened to his music, especially that record. I had spoken to the man, not the History, and that's whom I found on *Thirty-Three & 1/3*. I found a guy obsessed with wheels and speed (the references to 450s and 'stick shifties' in 'It's What You Value'); happy in his home at Friar Park (seen in Eric Idle's video for 'Crackerbox Palace'); tired of courtrooms and lawyers after being found guilty of 'unconscious plagarism' in the notorious 'My Sweet Lord' case ('This Song' delivered his own verdict); and so much in love with his future wife Olivia Arias that even the wide-open admiration of 'Beautiful Girl' was not testimony enough. He covered Cole Porter's song, 'True Love.'

Thirty-Three & 1/3 is also the sound of Harrison feeling absolutely free. It's all over the record in his sunny, doubled vocals and especially in his saucy bayou-county licks on 'Woman Don't You Cry for Me.' He founded Dark Horse Records in 1974 as a haven for himself and others, but it was not until he resolved legal difficulties with his original partner, A&M, and dissolved his final ties to EMI, that Harrison truly tasted independence. *Thirty Three & 1/3* was not only Harrison's best record since *All Things Must Pass*; it was the first time he could put his own name on his own label.

RUARY 7, 197

George Harrison To Record For Dark Horse; Signs With Own Label Handled By A&M

CANNES, France — MIDEM 1976 was the setting for George Harrison to announce that he had signed a multi-album deal with his own record label, Dark Horse Records.

The signing, revealed to **Cash Box** publisher George Albert, on hand for the MIDEM event, ends an association stretching back 14 years -- the start of the Beatles — with Capitol Records.

Harrison told Albert that the new contract is effective from January 27 and

*Harrison, Albert, Clyde, **CBs** Kim Thorne*

Dark Horse will continue to be distributed in the U.S. and Canada by A&M Records. A&M will also handle distribution of Dark Horse in the U.K.

Harrison's first Dark Horse album has already been completed and will be released in late spring throughout the world. Up to now Dark Horse had everything except Harrison product available to the label.

Harrison commented: "For the first time I feel I can receive personalized attention. I am very fond of Jerry Moss and his organization — it was shortly before the last MIDEM that I signed the first deal for Dark Horse with A&M — and I feel very secure creatively. I think that now I will be able to express all of my talents."

A&M president Moss and Dark Horse's Jonanthan Clyde from London were on hand to hear Harrison's announcement.

First singles to be released under the new deal are "From You To Us" by Stairsteps, produced by Bob Margouleff, Billy Preston and Stairsteps, and "Ain't Love Enough" by Attitudes, produced by Lee Keifer and the group.

son

solo career
shed by the
Things Must

ON JOINS ORSE

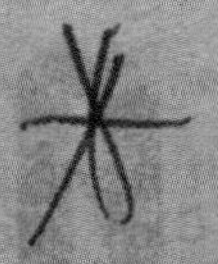

next album will be on his own Dark
nnounced at MIDEM, the music trade
ce, on Monday. And Mick Taylor has
in partnership with Colin Allen, the
with Focus.
EM this week discussing plans for Dark
epresentatives of A&M Records, which
hroughout the world. He officially joined
artist — on Tuesday.
m for the label will be released in late
cording plans, Harrison told the Melody
neone to produce me, either that or a
a friend working with me. I've found
can judge your own work. It's always
nd around.
et Ry Cooder to produce me. I've always

Harrison Quits EMI's Roster

By PETER JONES

CANNES—George Harrison has become the first of the ex-Beatles to formally break a 13-year association with EMI. He announced at MIDEM that his personal recording future would be on his own Dark Horse label which he formed 18

Of the other former Beatles, Paul McCartney has concluded a new world-wide deal with EMI, while John Lennon and Ringo Starr have still to confirm their future plans.

Harrison admitted that there had been no shortage of big money of-

By the time of *George Harrison*, he was the only act on the label. Yet in the thick of punk rock and the ascendance of hip hop, while the record business got drunk measuring an album's success in the tens of millions of copies sold, Harrison made, in the most literal sense, popular music. Of his five Dark Horse studio LPs during the Seventies and Eighties, all but *Gone Troppo* made *Billboard*'s Top Twenty and *Cloud Nine* hit the Top Ten.

Heard together now, the records seem like brothers, a boxed set originally issued in extended serial form. It has much to do with the attention to melody and concision in Harrison's guitar playing. Regardless of the circumstances – a Beatles song, his own albums, a guest lick or break on someone else's session – he made every note count. 'George, in the studio, would

spend a lot of time working out solos – nothing was done really fast,' Beatles engineer Geoff Emerick once said. Jeff Lynne saw that thoughtfulness firsthand, during the making of *Cloud Nine*: 'The guitar parts were meaningful pieces to him, right up there with the vocals. You could always remember one of his solos, because he put so much thought into them.' Listen to the liquid slide work in *George Harrison*'s 'Blow Away.' Or the sun-baked sigh of his dobro in *Gone Troppo*'s 'Greece' and the muscular clucking under Eric Clapton's quick, fierce screams in 'Wreck of the Hesperus' on *Cloud Nine*.

You can laugh and pray with Harrison – he does both in equal measures on these records – but much of his greatest songwriting was done in a spirit of worship and transformation. In a 1974 interview, during his first and only North American solo tour, Harrison responded to a question about identity – the weight of being Beatle George – this way: 'Gandhi says, 'Create and preserve the image of your choice." Harrison saw himself not as a star or a legend, but a man of questions, craft and surrender. The 'you' in many of his spiritual and romantic lyrics is rhetorical. They are songs of rigorous self-examination and shared prayer. He sang not from a pulpit, by right of celebrity, but from the ground, looking up, often on his knees.

On the very day I met him in 1976, while talking to a *Rolling Stone* writer, Harrison answered the inevitable Beatles-reunion query like this: 'The Beatles were other people a long time ago. They're for the history books, like the year 1492.' But the Beatles never stopped mattering completely to Harrison.
He often went back to his unrecorded songs and demos for these albums: 'See Yourself,'

'Not Guilty' and 'Circles' were all originally from The Beatles era. On the 1991 Japanese tour with Eric Clapton's band, caught on *Live in Japan*, he went even further back playing 'Old Brown Shoe' and 'Piggies,' complete with the comic, philharmonic coda. In 'When We Was Fab,' co-written with Jeff Lynne, Harrison cheerfully recreated the paisley-carnival air of 1967, with tongue firmly in cheek. And when Lennon died, 'All Those Years Ago' became the tender, healing centerpiece of *Somewhere in England*. Starr's loping drums were there; McCartney and his wife Linda added harmonies; and Harrison sang of a love that had survived success, hysteria, frustration and estrangement: 'Living with good and bad/I always looked up to you.' The Beatles had changed, defined and complicated Harrison's life. They were a huge part of his life, for better and worse – and he put everything on these records.

If you need any other reasons to forget all you think you know about Harrison's Dark Horse years, here are a couple of mine: 'Here Comes the Moon' is a gorgeous sequel to his *Abbey Road* classic 'Here Comes the Sun,' with milky-waterfall harmonies in the chorus line. Then there's the airtight, vocal-army introduction to 'Got My Mind Set on You,' his final number one hit and a cover of a 1962 R&B single by James Ray that Harrison had adored since the dawn of the Beatles.

But you will soon find your own pleasures. With the return of these songs and performances, in this very special set, love comes to everyone. Again.

David Fricke, November, 2003

ALL THOSE YEARS AGO

Words and Music by
GEORGE HARRISON

Em7
D
I'm talk-ing all a-bout how to give.
Instrumental
Em
Edim7
They don't act with much hon - es - ty.
But
D
F♯m7
Em7
Gm6
D
B7
you point the way to the truth when you say, "All you need is love."
End instrumental All those years a - go.
Em7
A
D
Em
Liv - ing with good and bad, I
Deep in the dark - est night, I

A
D
A
D
al - ways looked up to you. Now we're left cold and sad
send out a prayer to you. Now in the world of light
3
Em
A7
A7♯5
by some - one, the dev - il's best friend, some - one who of - fend - ed all.
where the spir - it free of the lies and all else that we de - spised.
D
We're liv - ing in a bad dream.
They've for - got - ten all a - bout God.
Em
Edim7
They've for - got - ten all a - bout man - kind. And
He's the on - ly rea - son we ex - ist. Yet

D
F♯m7
Em7
Gm6
3fr
3
you were the one they backed up to the wall
you were the one that they said was so weird
D
B7
Em7
D
F♯m7
all those years a - go.
all those years a - go.
You were the one who i -
You said it all, though not
Em7
Gm6
3fr
D
B7
1
Em7
mag - ined it all
man - y had ears,
all those years a - go.
all those years a - go.
2
Em7
D
F♯m7
Em7
Gm6
3fr
You had con - trol of our smiles and our tears

D
B7
Em7
A
all those years a - go.
D5
5fr
Em
Em7♭5
Gm6
3fr
D
F♯m7
Em7
Gm6
3fr
Ooh,
ooh.
D
B7
Repeat and Fade
Em7
Optional Ending
Em7
A
D
All those years a - go.

BABY DON'T RUN AWAY

Words and Music by
GEORGE HARRISON

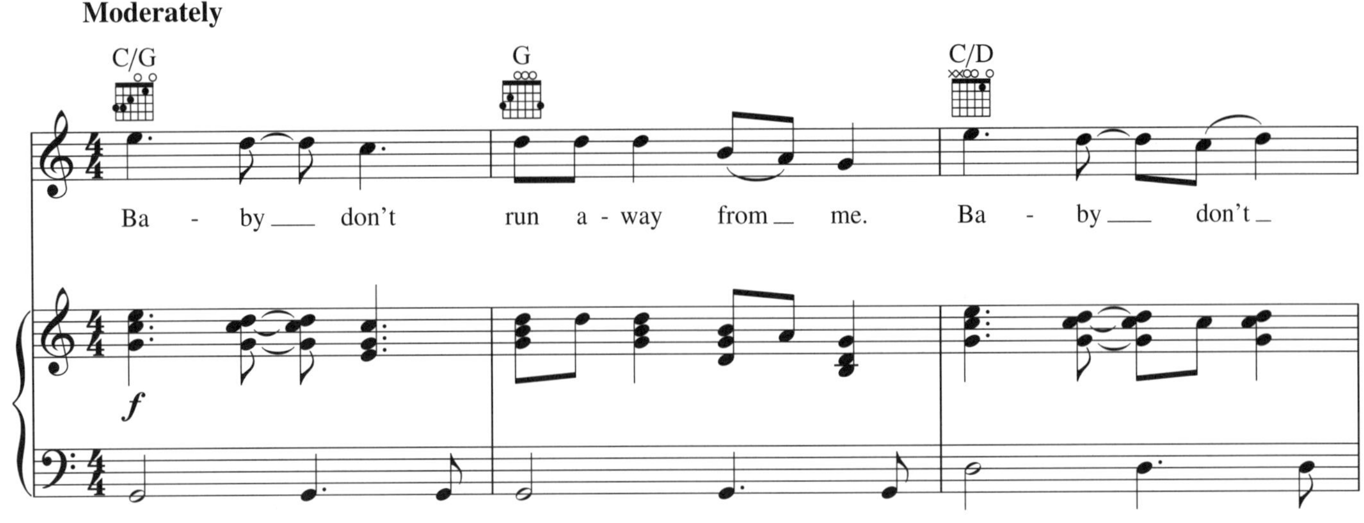

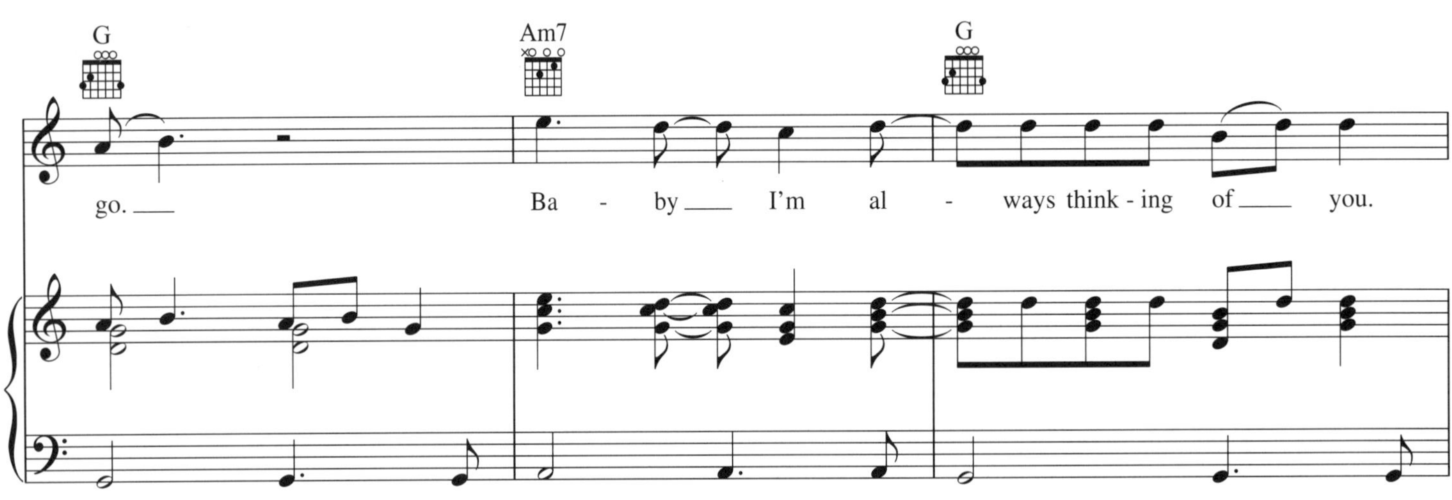

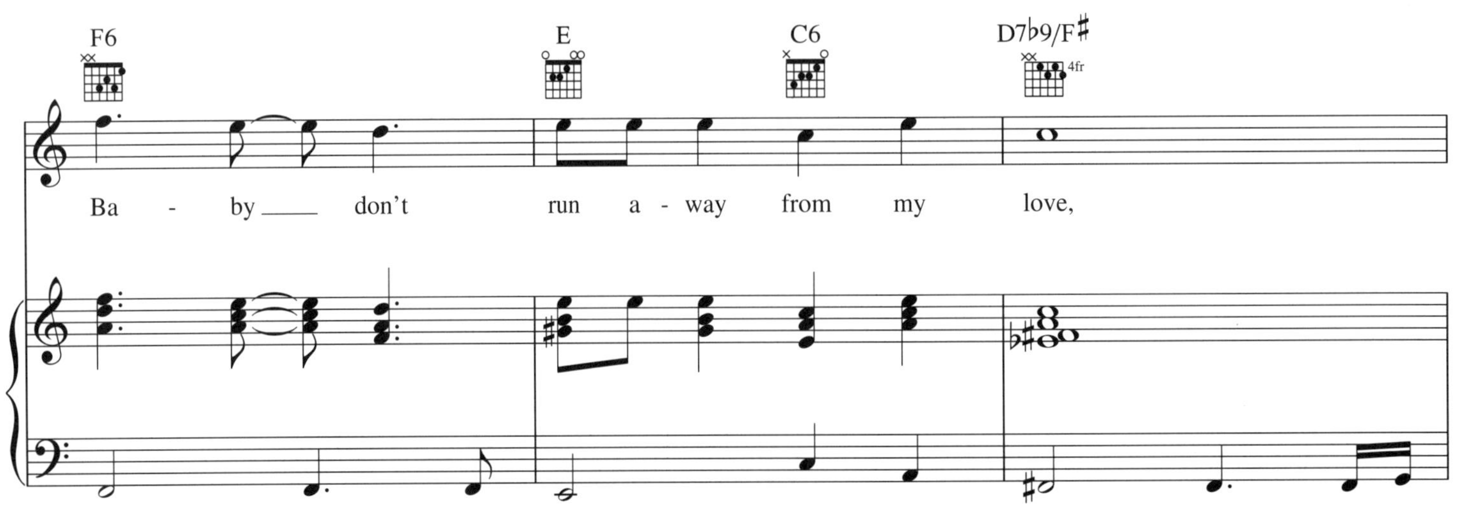

C
F/A
C
ooh.
C/G
G
C/D
You brought me ev - 'ry - thing I've want - ed. Lad - y don't
G
Am7
G/B
go. How could I ev - er live with - out you?
F6
E
C6
D7♭9/F♯
4fr
Lad - y don't run a - way from my love,

C
ooh.
G
D
G
Way out there where the o - cean is still, a calm re - flec - tion in the
Way back then it was eas - y to see a calm re - flec - tion in the
D
G
D
sea. Sat a - lone with the stars and the moon.
sea. Sitt - ing still and with - out an - y cares.
G
E7
Am
You turned 'round to me and love was in your
You turned out to be a lov - er who was

D
G
D/F♯
Em
eyes to see.
sure of me.
That's
Am
D
G
G/F♯
when it hap - pened to you and me.
Em
D
C
G/B
D/A
To Coda
C/G
G
C/D
Ba - by don't run a - way from me.
Ba - by don't

G
Am7
G
go.
Ba - by I'm al - ways think - ing of you.
F6
E
C6
D7♭9/F♯
4fr
Ba - by don't run a - way from my love,
C
ooh.
Run a - way from my
D7♭9/F♯
4fr
C
love.

D.S. al Coda
CODA
C/G
G
Ba - by don't run a - way from me.
C/D
G
Am7
Ba - by don't go.
Ba - by I'm al -
G
F6
E
C6
- ways think - ing of you.
Ba - by don't run a - way from my
D7♭9/F♯
4fr
C
love,
ooh.

1
2
D7♭9/F♯
4fr
Run a - way from my love.
C
Run a - way from my
D7♭9/F♯
4fr
love.
Gsus
3fr
G
Gsus2
G
C

BALTIMORE ORIOLE

Words and Music by HOAGY CARMICHAEL
and PAUL FRANCIS WEBSTER

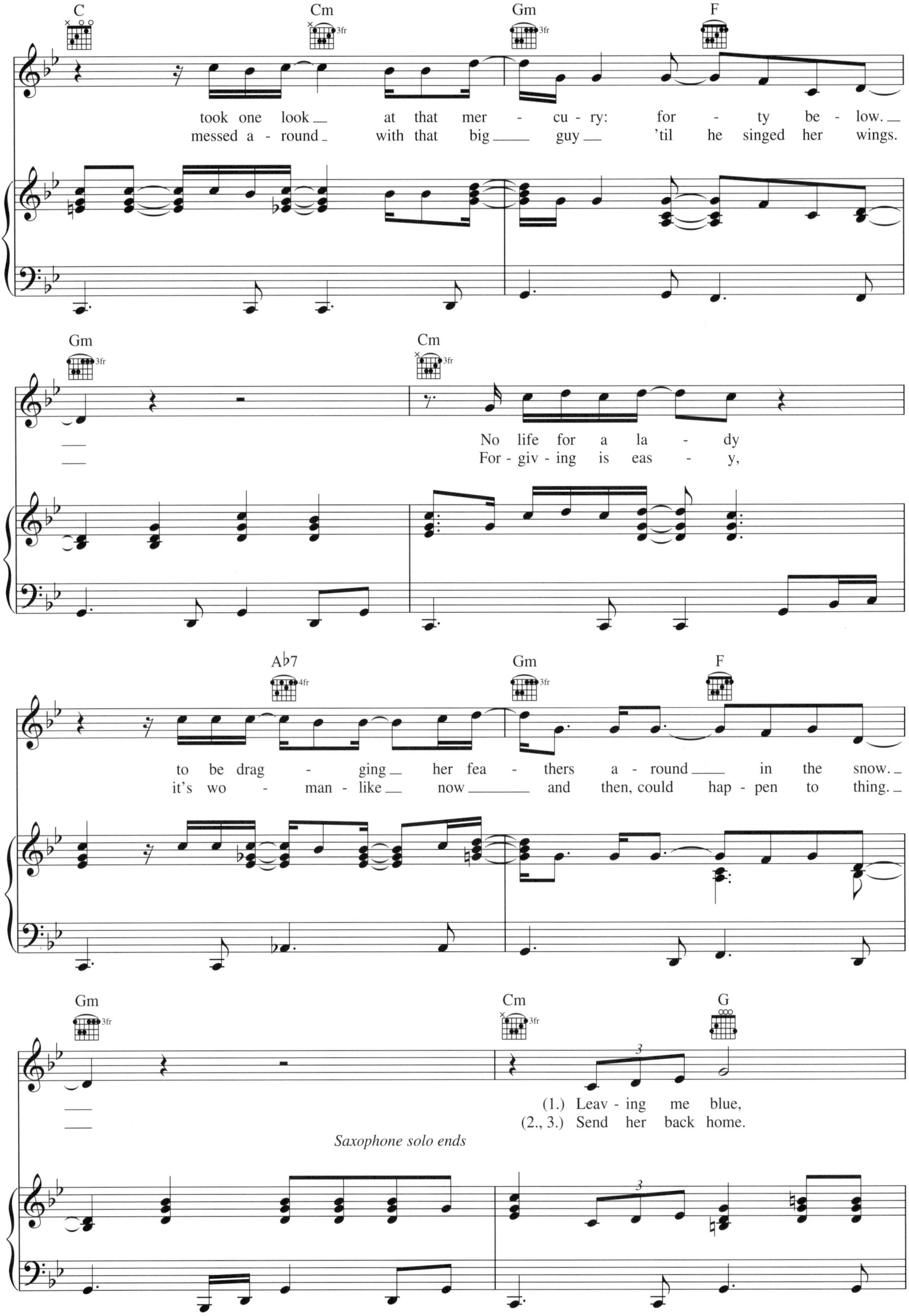
C
Cm
3fr
Gm
3fr
F
took one look at that mer - cu - ry: for - ty be - low.
messed a - round with that big guy 'til he singed her wings.
Gm
3fr
Cm
3fr
No life for a la - dy
For - giv - ing is eas - y,
A♭7
4fr
Gm
3fr
F
to be drag - ging her fea - thers a - round in the snow.
it's wo - man - like now and then, could hap - pen to thing.
Gm
3fr
Cm
3fr
G
(1.) Leav - ing me blue,
(2., 3.) Send her back home.
Saxophone solo ends

Cm
F
B♭
D7
off she flew to the Tan - gi - pa - ho, down in Lou - i - si - an - a.
Home ain't home with-out her war - bl - ing. How she can
Gm
Gm/F
1
Cm
E♭7
where a two - tim - ing jay - bird met the di - vine Miss O.
sing. Make a lone - ly man hap -
D7
D7sus
D7
I'd like to ruf - fle his plum - age. That
2,3
Cm
E♭7
D7
Gm
Gm/F
To Coda
py, Bal - ti - more O - ri - ole,

E♭7
D7♭9
4fr
D.S. al Coda
3
come down from that
CODA
E♭7
D7♭9
4fr
come down from that bough.
Gm
3fr
Gm/F
E♭7
D7♭9
4fr
Fly to your dad - dy now.
Gm
3fr
C
Cm
3fr
Instrumental solo
Gm
3fr
F
Gm
3fr

Cm
Ab7
Gm
F
Gm
Cm
G+
Cm
F
Bb
D7
Gm
Gm/F
Cm
Eb7
D7
Repeat ad lib. and Fade
Optional Ending
Gm
Gm/F
Eb7
D7b9
Gm

BLOOD FROM A CLONE

Words and Music by
GEORGE HARRISON

D
A
D
A
D
You need some oom - pah- pah, noth - ing like Frank Zap- pa.
There seems a con - fu - sion, un - der the il - lu -sion
Don't want no mu - sic, but they're mak-ing you sick_with
A
D
A
E
And not New Wave.___ They don't play that crap. Try
that they know just ___ what will suit you all.
some aw - ful nois - es that they get played by
C
G
beat - ing your head ___ on a brick ___ wall,
Beat - ing my head ___ on a brick ___ wall,
beat - ing their heads ___ on a brick ___ wall,

D
E
A
hard like a stone.
hard like a stone.
hard like a stone.
C
G
Don't have time for the mu - sic. They want the
Ain't got time for the mu - sic. They want the
Ain't no mess - ing 'round with mu - sic. Give them the
B♭
A
D
G
D
G
D
G
blood from a clone.
blood from a clone.
blood from a clone.
D
G
1.2.
D
3.
D

A
D
A
D
Where will it all — lead us? I thought we had freed us
A
D
A
E
D
A
D
from the mun-dane. Seems I'm wrong a - gain. Could be they lack roots. They're
A
D
A
D
A
E
still wear-ing jack-boots. They're march-ing some-where in the pour-ing rain.
Three times
C
G
D
E
Beat-ing my head — on a brick — wall, hard — like a stone.

A
C
G
Don't have time for the mu-sic. They want the
Ain't no mess - ing 'round with mu-sic. Give them the
Ain't no time for the mu-sic. They want the
B♭
A
D
G
D
G
D
G
blood from a clone.
D
G
D
Repeat and fade
A
D
A
D
A
D
A
E

BEAUTIFUL GIRL

Words and Music by
GEORGE HARRISON

E
E7
A
eyes.
Not the kind you go hand-
Dm6
A
Dm6
ing a - round,
want to keep her right there.
A
Dm6
E
E7
But this love, it don't come as no sur-prise.
D
E7
A
E
And when I saw the way that she smiled at me,
And then I saw the way that she smiled at me,

D
E7
A
E
I knew it there and then that she was A - one.
I knew it there and then that she was A - one.
And then I felt the way she was touch - ing me
And when I felt the way she got through to me
was some-thing I had known I was wait - ing up - on.
was some-thing I had known I was wait - ing up - on.

A
Dm6
A
Nev - er seen such a beau - ti - ful girl; had me quick - ly un - tied.
Nev - er seen such a beau - ti - ful girl; got me shak - ing in - side,
Dm6
A
Dm6
Call - ing to me she made me re - al - ize.
call - ing on me from deep with - in her eyes.
E
E7
A
Not the kind that is lost
Not the kind you go hand -
Dm6
A
Dm6
or is found, she has al - ways been there,
ing a - round, want to keep her right there.

A
Dm6
E
E7
To Coda
a lov - er need - ed for this soul to sur - vive.
But this love, it don't come
A
Dm6
A
Dm6
A
Dm6
1. E
E7
2. E
E7
E9
D.S. al Coda
Coda
Dm6
E
E7
as no sur - prise.

A
Dm6
A
Dm6
A
Dm6
E
A
Dm6
A
Dm6
A
Dm6
E
E7
E
E7
A

BLOW AWAY

Words and Music by
GEORGE HARRISON

F♯m7
A7sus4
A7
A7sus4
A7
A - bout_ to go down,__ I had al - most for - got.
In - stant am - ne - sia,__ Yang to the Yin.
The mo - ment had passed__ like I knew that it should.
cresc.
D
Bm
F♯m
A7sus4
A7
D
Bm
All I got to do is to, to love you. All I got to be is__
mf
C
G
F♯m
Bm
F♯m
A
be hap - py. All it's got to take is some warmth to make_ it blow a -
F
C
A7sus4
A7
way, blow a - way,__ blow a - way.

D
Bm
F♯m
A7sus4
A7
D
Bm
All I got to do is to, to love you. All I got to be is
C
G
F♯m
Bm
F♯m
A
be hap - py. All it's got to take is some warmth to make it blow a -
F
C
G
D
F
C
way, blow a - way, blow a - way.
A7sus4
1. 2.
A7
3.
A7
D.S. 𝄋
and fade

BREATH AWAY FROM HEAVEN

Words and Music by
GEORGE HARRISON

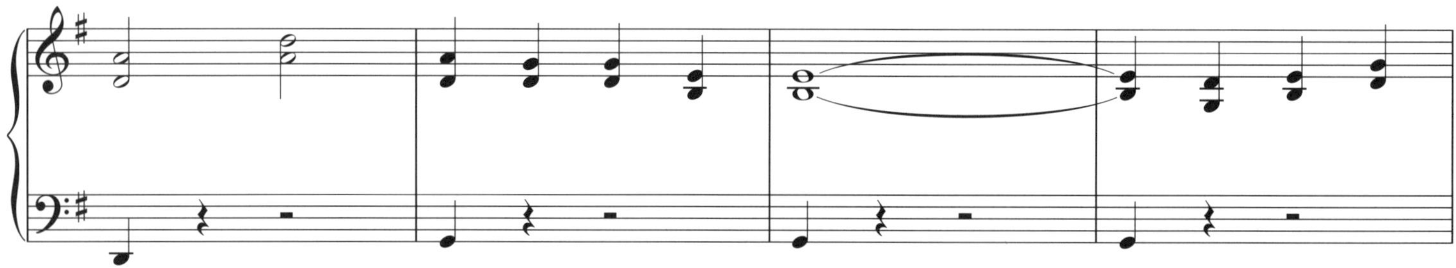

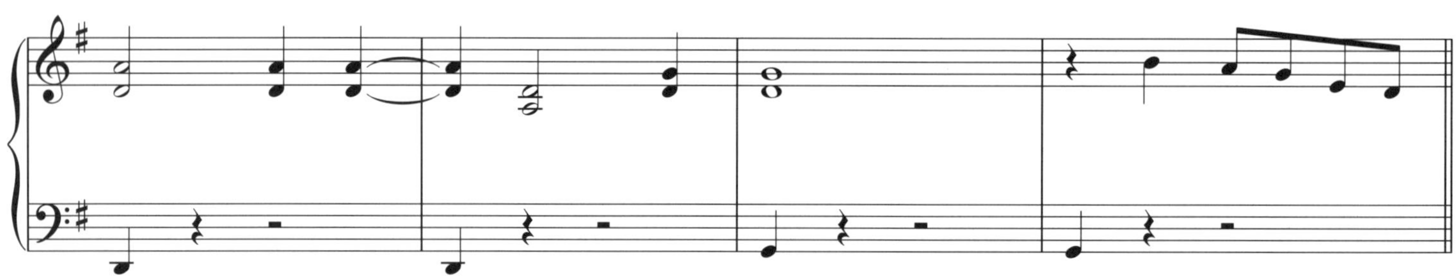

a sigh,
as the morn - ing
light
was paint - ing
whis - pers of a joy.
G
Bm/F♯
And I was in the can - dle - lit
Solo ends
And I was cap - tured by her lone -
Em
G/D
Bm
bed - room,
li - ness,

G
Bm/F♯
Em
G/D
Bm
en - chant - ing beau - ty shim - mer - ing mag - ic - 'lly,
a wound - ed ti - ger on a wil - low - y path,
Am
like an ir - i - des - cent cloud be - ing blown by a wes - ter - ly
like an o - pal - es - cent moon all a - lone in the sky of a for -
C
N.C.
To Coda
wind. Mm. She can move your
- eign land. Mm.
soul with - out you know - ing.

She can take the breath a - way from heav - en.
Ooh, ah.
D.S. al Coda
CODA
She can take the breath
a - way from heav - en.

She can move your soul ___ with - out ___ you know - ing.
She is like an ev - er - last - ing blos - som.

She can take the breath ___ a - way ___ from

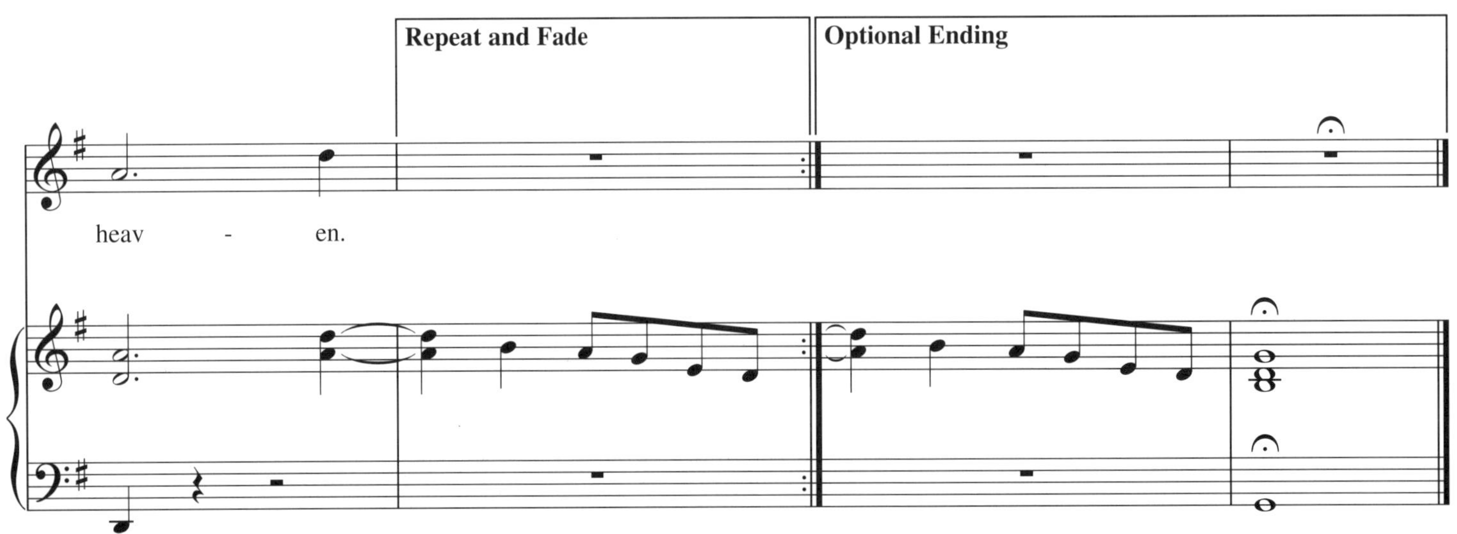
Repeat and Fade
Optional Ending
heav - en.

CHEER DOWN

Words and Music by GEORGE HARRISON
and TOM PETTY

D
And the smile on your face
is some - times out of place.
C
Gm
3fr
Don't
mind; no frowns. Cheer down.
Gm
A
Gm6
If your hair should fall,

Gm6
3fr
if your shares should crash,
When your teeth drop out,
D
Gm6
3fr
you'll get by
you'll get by
D
A
3
e - ven with - out get - ting a rash.
e - ven with - out tak - ing a bite.
There's no tears
If your doc
D
C
to be shed;
should be dead,
I'm gon - na love you in - stead.
I'm gon - na love you in - stead.

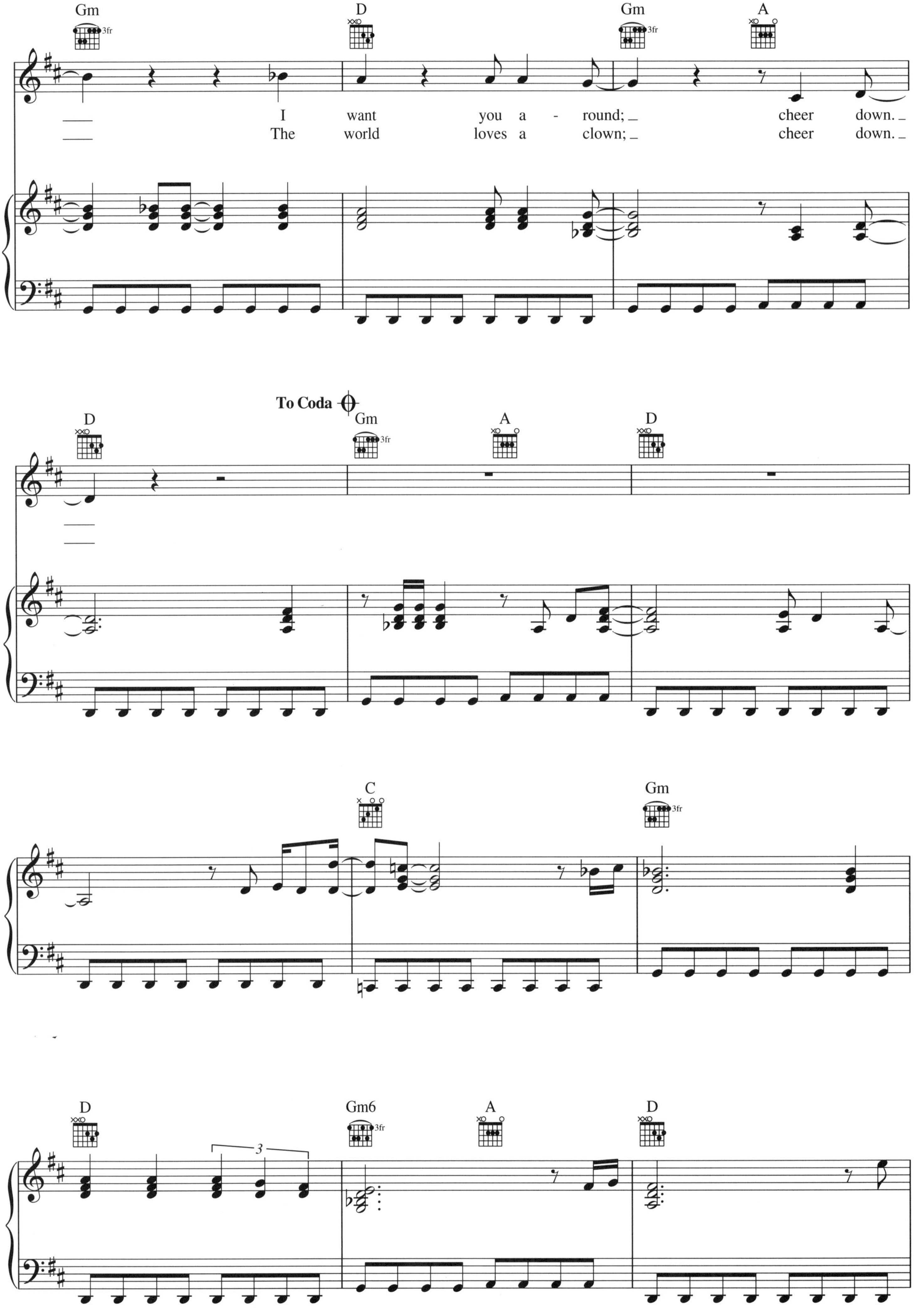

Gm D Gm A

I want you a - round; cheer down.
The world loves a clown; cheer down.

To Coda

D Gm A D

C Gm

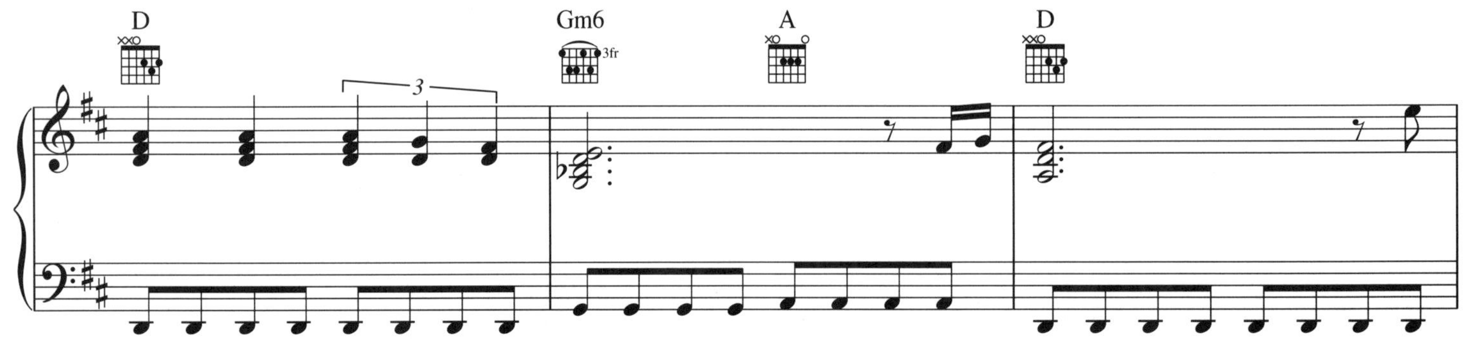

D.S. al Coda
CODA
Gm
3fr
D
I want you a - round;
Gm
3fr
A
D
cheer down.
Gm6
3fr
A
D
Gm6
3fr
A
D
Play 11 times ad lib.

CRACKERBOX PALACE

Words and Music by
GEORGE HARRISON

E♭
6 fr.
B♭
F
Gm
3 fr.
F
E♭
6 fr.
they said: I wel-come you to Crack-er-box Pal-ace;
Some-one said: While you're a part of Crack-er-box Pal-ace,
And we wel-come you to Crack-er-box Pal-ace;
B♭
F
Dm
E♭
6 fr.
F
we've been ex-pect-ing you.
do what the rest all do
we've been ex-pect-ing you.
You'll bring such joy in
or face the fact that
You'll bring such joy in
Gm
3 fr.
F
E♭
6 fr.
E♭m7
6 fr.
1. 2.
B♭
F
Crack-er-box Pal-ace; no mat-ter where you roam, know our love is true.
Crack-er-box Pal-ace may have no oth-er choice than to de-port you.
Crack-er-box Pal-ace; no mat-ter where you roam, know our love is
Gm
3fr.
F
E♭
6fr.
E♭m7
6fr.
3.
B♭
F
Cm
3 fr.
true.

B♭
F
Cm
3 fr.
B♭
F
Cm
3 fr.
B♭
F
Cm
3 fr.
B♭
F7
B♭
Gm
3 fr.
F
Cm
3 fr.
E♭
6 fr.
B♭
Gm
3 fr.
F
Cm
3fr.
Some times are good; some times are bad.
That's all a part of life.
E♭
6 fr.
B♭
Gm
3 fr.
F
Cm
3 fr.
E♭
6fr.
B♭
Gm
3 fr.
F
Cm
3fr.
And stand-ing in be-tween them all
I met a Mis-ter Grief,

E♭
6 fr.
B♭
F
Gm
3 fr.
F
E♭
6 fr.
and he said: I welcome you to Crack-er-box Pal-ace;
wel-come you to Crack-er-box Pal-ace;
B♭
F
Dm
E♭
6 fr.
F
was not ex-pect-ing you.
we've been ex-pect-ing you.
Let's rap and tap at
You'll bring such joy in
Gm
3 fr.
F
E♭
6 fr.
E♭m7
6 fr.
To Coda
Crack-er-box Pal-ace; know that the Lord is well and in-side of you.
Crack-er-box Pal-ace; no mat-ter where you roam, know our love is true.
B♭
F
Gm
3 fr.
F
E♭
6 fr.
E♭m7
6 fr.
D.S. al Coda
And we

Coda
B♭
F
Gm
3 fr.
F
E♭
6 fr.
B♭
F
Dm
E♭
6 fr.
F
Gm
3 fr.
F
E♭
6 fr.
E♭m7
6 fr.
You'll bring such joy in Crack-er-box Pal-ace; no mat-ter where you roam,
know our love,
know our love is true.
B♭
F
Gm
3 fr.
F
E♭
6 fr.
E♭m7
6 fr.
B♭

CIRCLES

Words and Music by
GEORGE HARRISON

Csus C Bsus/F♯ Bsus B

De - cide he was a swine as you go round and round in

Em 𝄋 G Gmaj7/F♯

cir - cles. He who knows does not

G7/F G6/E Am Am(maj7)/G♯ Am7/G Am6/F♯

speak. He who speaks does not know. {And I know that / And}

Dm B♭ Bm Bm/D

I go round in cir - cles.

To Coda 𝄌

Fm/C
Csus/G
Dis - like some - one and will not bend.
Lat - er they may be - come your
C/E
C
Bsus/F♯
Esus2
B/D♯
B
best friend as life it goes a - round in
Em
Fm/C
Fm
Csus/G
C
cir - cles.
Bsus/F♯
Esus2
B/D♯
B
Em
Those cir - cles.

Fm/C
Fm
Csus/G
C
Bsus/F♯
4fr
Esus2
B/D♯
4fr
B
Em
D.S. al Coda
Those cir - cles.
CODA
Fm/C
Fm
Soul takes on a bod - y, with each birth we make our date. With
Csus
3fr
C
Bsus
life and death a - long the road, the soul re - in - car - nates. The show goes round and round

B
Em
in cir - cles.
Fm/C
Fm
Csus/G
C
Bsus/F♯
4fr
Esus2
When loss and gain and up and down
be - comes the same, then
B/D♯
4fr
B
Em
we stop go'n in cir - cles.
Bsus/F♯
4fr
Esus2
B/D♯
4fr
B
Em
Round and round
in
those
cir - cles.

Bsus/F♯
4fr
Esus2
B/D♯
4fr
B
Round and round and round those
Em
1
2
cir - cles.
Those
Bsus/F♯
4fr
Esus2
B/D♯
4fr
B
Em
cir - cles.
(Lead vocal ad lib. on repeat)
Those cir - cles.
Optional Ending
Bsus/F♯
4fr
Esus2
B/D♯
4fr
B
Em
Repeat and Fade

CLOUD NINE

Words and Music by
GEORGE HARRISON

Join my dream, tell me yes. Bail out should there be a mess. The
Take my smile and my heart; they were yours from the start. The
Dm
Gm
3fr
pieces you don't need are mine.
pieces to omit are mine.
1
F/G
Gm
N.C.
Take my
2
Have my
love;
hope,
use it while it does
maybe even share
you good.
a joke.
Share my highs, but the times that he hurts,
If there's good to be shown, you may make

Dm
pay no mind. These piec - es you don't need are mine.
it all your own. And if you want to quit, that's fine,
Gm
3fr
Dm
I'll see you there on Cloud Nine.
while you're out look - ing for Cloud Nine.
Gm
3fr
Fmaj7
Gm7
N.C.
Gm
3fr
Instrumental solo

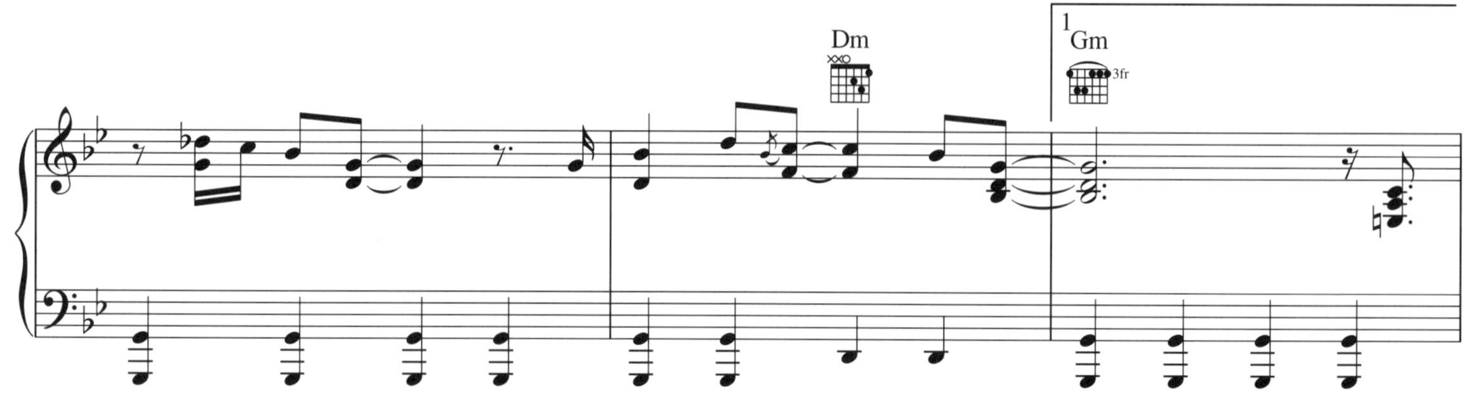
Dm
1
Gm
3fr

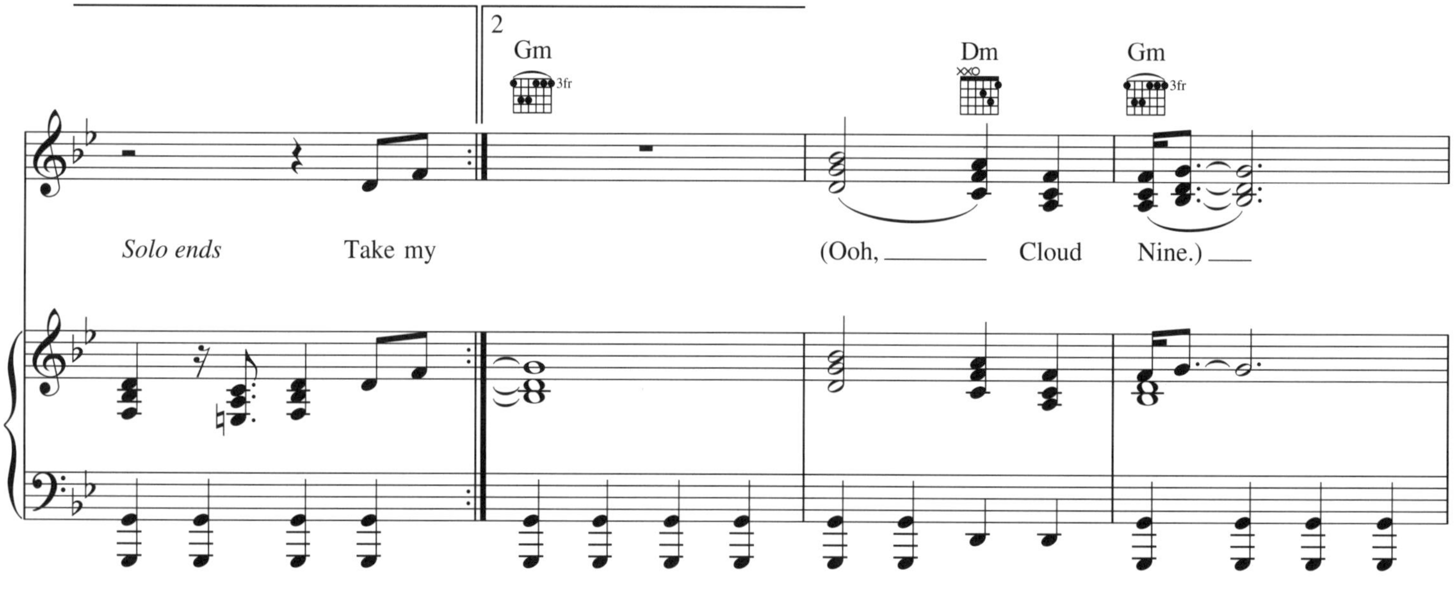
2
Gm
3fr
Dm
Gm
3fr
Solo ends
Take my
(Ooh, Cloud Nine.)

DARK SWEET LADY

Words and Music by
GEORGE HARRISON

A13
D
I've real - ly fall - en.
D/C♯
Bm
F♯
Bm
C9
You came_ and helped_ me through_ when I'd_ let go._
D
D/C♯
Bm
F♯
Bm
You came_ from out_ the blue._
C9
A13
D.S. 𝄋 al Coda 𝄌
Nev-er_ have known_ what_ I'd done with - out you._

Coda
A13
C9
and I love you dear - ly,
A13
C9
my dark, sweet la - dy.
A13
F♯7+5
D
Slower

DEAR ONE

Words and Music by
GEORGE HARRISON

A
A7
D (add E)
2 fr.
E7
E7sus4
Re - born, world - wise,
A
D
mind at rest.
A
A7
D (add E)
2 fr.
E7
E7sus4
True heart sow you,
Dear One show me
(mp)
A
D (add E)
2 fr.
A
God has blessed. Your
sim - ple Grace. Move

A7
D (add E)
2 fr.
E7
E7sus4
soul
whis - pers,
me
toward Thee
A
D
No chord
love con - fessed.
with each pace.
E7
A
E7
My spir - it sings to you now; cre - a - tion stands
mf
A
E7
A
at your feet. My feel - ings call to you now;

E7
A
E7
Dear One, I love (a) you.
You hear my spir-
A
E7
A
it sing to you; you see cre - a - tion at your feet.
E7
A
E7
You feel my feel - ings call - ing you; you know, Dear One,
A
D (add E)
2 fr.
To Coda
I love (a) you.

A
A7
D
A
A7
D
A
D
E
D.S. 𝄋 al Coda 𝄌
Coda
A
A7
D
A
A7
D
A
D
E
A
A7
D
A

DEVIL'S RADIO

Words and Music by
GEORGE HARRISON

E
C♯m
4fr
B
G♯m
4fr
like vul-tures swoop - ing down be - low on the
with gos - sip broad - cast to and fro on the
1
B
E
dev - il's ra - di - o.
2
B
dev - il's ra - di - o.
E
G
B5
G
E
G
(Oh yeah, gos - sip. Gos -
B5
G
E
C♯m
4fr
B
sip, oh yeah.)
He's in the clubs and bars,
He's in your T. - V. set;

E
A
B
E
and nev - er turns it down
won't give it a rest.
That
C#m
4fr
B
G#m
4fr
1 B
talk - in' a - bout what he don't know on the dev - il's ra - di - o.
soul - be - tray - ing so - and - so,
E
2 B
E
G
the dev - il's ra - di - o.
(Gos -
B5
G
E
G
B5
G
sip, gos - sip. Gos - sip, gos -

E
G
B5
G
E
G
Gos - sip,
oh yeah,
sip. Oh yeah, gos - sip. Gos -
B5
G
E
A
oh yeah,
gos - sip.
It's white and black, like in -
sip, oh yeah.)
E
dus - tri - al waste, pol - lu - tion of the high - est de - gree.
A
You won - der why I don't

B
N.C.
hang out much; I wonder how you can't see.
C♯m
B
E
A
B
4fr
He's in the films and songs, and all your mag - a - zines.
E
C♯m
B
G♯m
It's ev - 'ry - where that you may go, the
B
E
C♯m
B
devil's ra - di - o.
Guitar solo

E
A
B
E
C♯m
4fr
B
G♯m
4fr
B
E
G
B5
G
Solo ends
(Oh
yeah,
gos -
E
G
B5
G
E
sip.
Gos - sip,
oh
yeah.)

A

Runs thick and fast, and no one real - ly sees quite

E

what bad it can do,

A B

as it shapes you in - to some - thing cold, like an Es - ki - mo ig - loo.

N.C. C♯m B E

It's all a - cross our lives;
Can creep up in the dark, make

A
B
E
like a weed, it's spread till
us hide be - hind shades, and
C♯m
B
G♯m
1
B
noth - ing else has space to grow, the dev - il's ra - di - o.
buzz - ing like a dy - na - mo,
E
2 B
E
G
the dev - il's ra - di - o. (Gos -
B5
G
E
G
B5
G
Oh yeah, oh yeah. Gos - sip,
sip, gos - sip. Gos - sip, gos -

E
G
B5
G
E
G
gos - sip. __
I heard you on the se - cret _ wire - less,
sip.
Oh yeah,
gos - sip.
Gos -
B5
G
E
G
you know, the dev - il's ra - di - o, ____ child.
sip,
oh
yeah.
Gos -
B5
G
E
G
B5
G
sip,
gos - sip.
Gos - sip,
gos -
E
N.C.
sip.)

DREAM AWAY

Words and Music by
GEORGE HARRISON

Bm
Em
Em/D
F7
eye ay. Sy - a te lee ay vee show.
Bm
Em
Em/D
Mid - night sun - shine si - lent thun - der. Sky
Wak - ing while you're still deep sleep - ing. Find -
Greed - y feel - ing, wheel - ing deal - ing. Los -
F7
N.C.
as black as day.
- ing you're not here.
- ing what you won.
E♭
3fr
F
1
G
On - ly a dream a - way.
Oh ry in
Watch-ing a dream ap - pear.
See the dream come un - done.

2, 3
G
E♭
3fr
F
G
C
G
Tum - bl - ing through a thou - sand cen - tur - ies.
Stum - ble you may with the el - e - men - tar - y.
D
E♭
3fr
F
G
You don't know where you'll land. It's so dark
Luck - y you got so far. All you owe
C
G
D
in my - thol - o - gy.
is a - pol - o - gies.

E♭ 3fr
F
G
Treas - ures of his - to - ry to be found
Meas - ure the mys - ter - y and as - tound
C
G
C
near the leg - ends of time. All the
with - out tak - ing up time. Still the
G
C
Am
To Coda
hand - i - works re - main there.
hand - i - works re - main there.
E♭ 3fr
F
G
D.S. al Coda
(take 2nd ending)
On - ly a dream a - way. Oh ry in

CODA
E♭
3fr
F
G
On - ly a dream a - way.
D
Oh ry in eye ay. Oh ry in
Bm
Em
Em/D
C
D7
eye ay. Oh ry in eye key ooh lay. Ka Lay ooh
G
D
Bm
Em
Em/D
lau ee. Oh ry in eye ay. Say - a te lee ay vee show.

F7
Bm
Em
Em/D
In out, hot cold, up down, young old. What
a lot to do.
N.C.
E♭
3fr
F
G
Shar-ing a dream with you.
Oh ry in
eye ay. Oh ry in eye ay. Oh ry in
D

Em
Em/D
C
D7
G
D
eye key ooh lay.
Ka Lay ooh lau ee. Oh ry in
Bm
Em
Em/D
F7
D/F♯
Play 3 times
eye ay. Sy - a te lee ay vee show.
Oh ry in
G
D
Bm
Em
Em/D
eye ay. Oh ry in eye ay. Oh ry in eye key ooh lay.
C
D7
G
D
Bm
Ka Lay ooh lau ee. Oh ry in eye ay.

FASTER

Words and Music by
GEORGE HARRISON

A
Dsus4
D
Dsus2
Peo-ple be-came his friend.
is noth-ing left to spare.
Now they stood and no-
Still the crowds came pour-
ticed him;
ing in.
want-ed to be a part of it.
Some had hoped to see him fail.
Bm
Pulled out some poor ma-chin-er-y. So he worked till the piec-es
Fill-ing their hearts with jeal-ous-ies, cra-zy peo-ple with love so
fit.
frail.
The peo-ple were in-
The peo-ple were in-
No need to won-der

G
D
Bm
trigued. His wife held back her fears.
The head-lines gave ac -
trigued. His wife held back her fears.
The head-lines gave ac -
why. His wife held back her fears.
So few have e - ven
G
D
A/C#
Bm
A
claim. He'd re - al - ized their dreams.
claim. He'd re - al - ized their dreams.
tried to re - al - ize their dreams.
A(no 3rd)
C
G
D
A
Bm
Fast - er than a bul - let from a gun,
he is fast - er than ev - 'ry - one.
G
A(no 3rd)
C
G
Quick - er than the blink - ing of an eye,
like a flash,

D
A
Bm
D
you could miss him go-ing by.
No one knows quite how he does it, but it's
A
F♯m
Bm
To Coda
true, they say: He's the mas - ter of go - ing fast - er.
G
1.
Dsus4
D
2.
Dsus4
D
D.S. al Coda
Coda
A(no 3rd)
C
G
D
A

FISH ON THE SAND

Words and Music by
GEORGE HARRISON

A5
C
G
I see you in love;
You know I feel the pain;
C
F
Am/E
I see you in the moon a-bove.
I'm tired of play-ing games with you,
But I want to know that you've not
though there's noth - ing else at once
Dm
A5
C
lost the sight of me.
that would set me free.
A5
C
A5
You know I need you;
You know I love you;

C
A5
5fr
C
you know I love you.
you know I need you.
If I'm not with you, I'm
If I can't be with you, I'm
F
G
C
not so much of a man; I'm like a fish on the sand.
1
2
N.C.
E/G♯
No use to no
Am
one else; I'm all dried up,
N.C.

F
Db
N.C.
watch ing all our lives go by.
I can't be-lieve you want to see
G/B
C
G
me cry - ing. I hold you in my heart;
C
F
Am/E
I know that you're a part of me.
But it's a must to know
Dm
A5
5fr
C
that you love me too.
I look you in the eye;

G
C
F
you're swim-ming by my tear - drops.
Am/E
Dm
A5
5fr
But I want to know for sure that you'll let me see.
C
A5
5fr
C
You know I want you;
You know I need you;
A5
5fr
C
A5
5fr
you know I need you.
you know I love you.

C
F
1
G
If I'm not with you, I'm not so much of a man; I'm like a fish on the sand.
2
I'm a fish on the sand.
Not so much of a man,
more a fish on the sand.

GONE TROPPO

Words and Music by
GEORGE HARRISON

F/C
C
He smile, mu - cho in a sun-shine.
Good time, drink - ing on me bot-tle.
Night life,
The high wide
G
C
F
count-ing de fruit bat.
more-ton bay fig.
Trop-po,
gone
C
F
trop-po.
Trop-po,
it's
C
G
C
C
F/C
C
time you know I gone trop - po.

G
C
F/C
Plant me in
Quite like, you
C
G
C
de hel - i - con - a.
No thank,
meet - ing de peo - ples.
ain't seen a sun - set.
Could be
liv - ing in rain hill.
F/C
C
Wake me, eat - a the pa - pa - ya.
Much hot, not
Sun hot, you don't got a back - ache.
Brown skin and
G
C
F
much on the bod - y.
Trop - po,
gone
ver - y a peel - ing.

C
F
trop - po.
Trop - po,
Gone trop - po,
To Coda
C
G
C
it's time you know I gone trop - po.
F/C
C
G
C
(Guitar solo ad lib.)
F/C
C
G
C
D.S. al Coda

CODA
F
-po. Oh, trop-po, gone
C
F
trop-po. Trop-po, it's
C
G
C
F/C
time you know I gone trop - po.
C
G
C

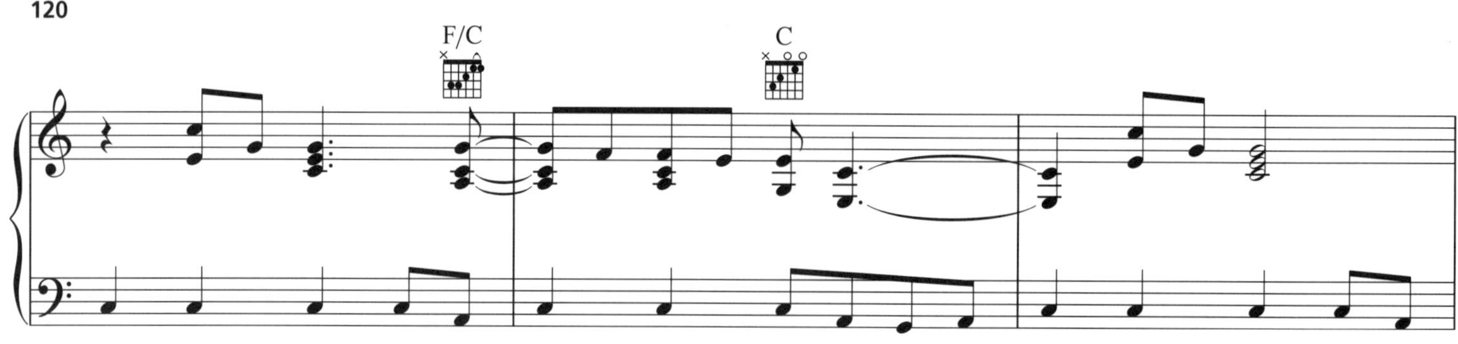
F/C
C

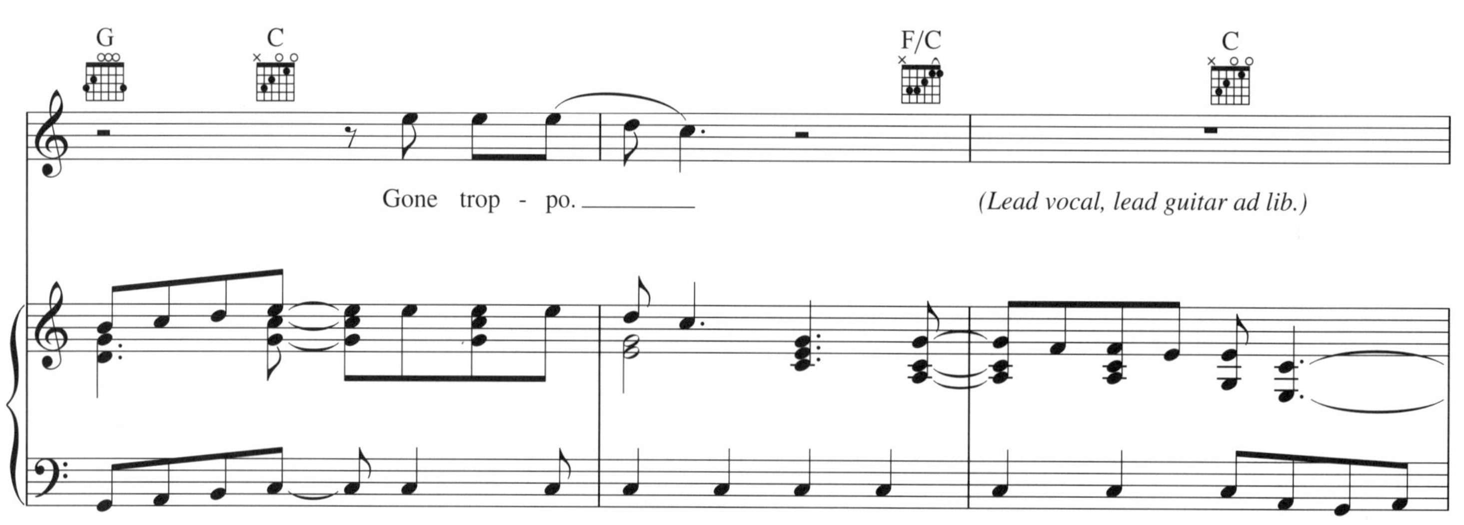
G
C
F/C
C
Gone trop - po.
(Lead vocal, lead guitar ad lib.)

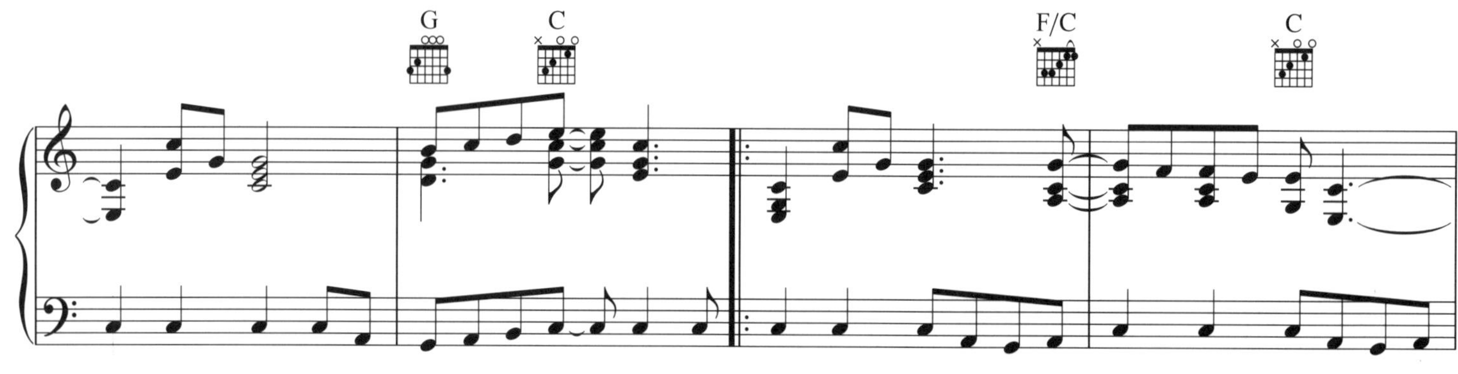
G
C
F/C
C

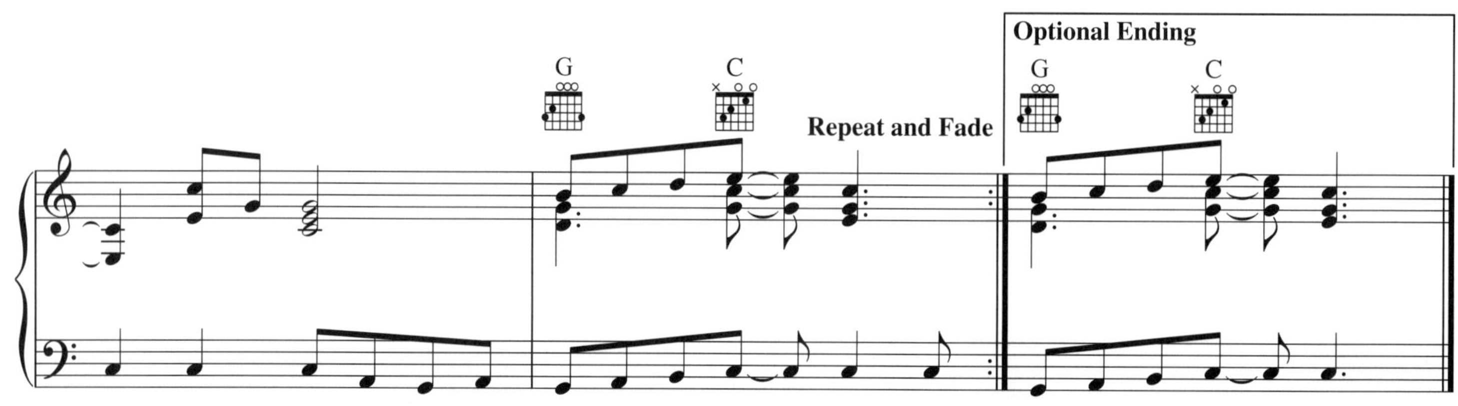
G
C
Repeat and Fade
Optional Ending
G
C

GOT MY MIND SET ON YOU

Words and Music by
RUDY CLARK

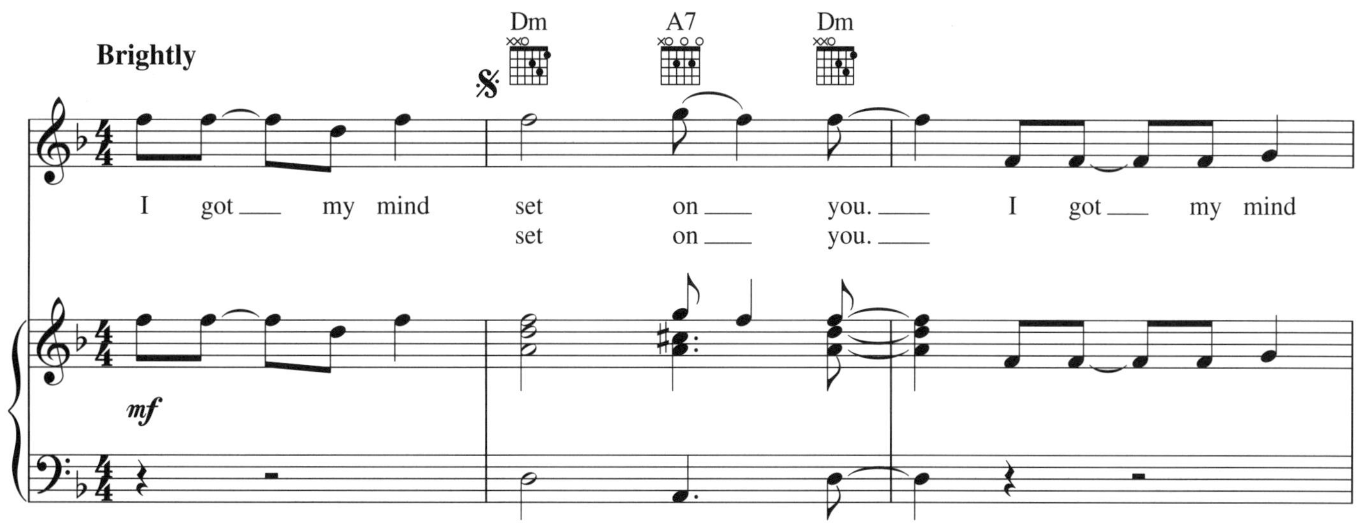

B♭
C
F
B♭
ey, a whole lot - ta spend - ing mon - ey.
C
F
B♭
C
It's gon - na take plen - ty of mon - ey to do it right,
3
3
F
B♭
C
F
B♭
child. It's gon - na take time,
C
F
B♭
C
a whole lot - ta pre - cious time. It's gon - na take

F
B♭
C
F
B♭
pa - tience and time, mm, to do it, to do it, to
F
B♭
To Coda I
To Coda II
F
B♭
F
do it, to do it, to do it, to do it right, child.
Dm
A7
Dm
I got my mind set on you. I got my mind
F
C7
F
Dm
A7
Dm
set on you. I got my mind set on you.

F
C7
F
I got my mind set on you.
And
B♭
F
this time I know it's real, the feel - ing that I feel.
B♭
F
B♭
I know if I put my mind to it, I
F
C
D.S. al Coda I
know that I real - ly can do it.
I got my mind
3
3

CODA I
F
B♭
F
do it, to do it right.
Dm
A7
Dm
F
C7
F
Dm
A7
Dm
F
C7
F
I got my mind

Dm
A7
Dm
F
C7
F
set on you. I got my mind set on you.
I got my mind set on you. I got my mind
set on you. And this time I know it's real,
Bb
the feel - ings that I feel. I

F
B♭
F
know if I put my mind to it. I know that I real - ly can do it.
C
D.S.S. al Coda II
But it's gon - na take mon -
CODA II
F
B♭
F
do it, to do it right.
Repeat and Fade
Optional Ending
Dm
A7
Dm
F
C7
F
Set on you.
Set on you.

I REALLY LOVE YOU

Words and Music by
LEROY SWEARINGEN

Bm
E7
A
E
ahh.
Yeah,
A
C♯m
Bm
E7♭9
A
C♯m
you,
you,
I real - ly, real - ly love you.
I real - ly, real - ly want you.
4fr
Bm
E7♭9
A
C♯m
Bm
E7♭9
No - bod - y else will do.
That's why I love you. That's
A
1
E
2
A E
why, why, why. Yeah
why. Well,

D
A
babe you know I love you so. I'd pay the world if
A7
D
you could know. (And / But) when I see you com - in' down the street my
Bm
E7
E7#5
A
C#m
4fr
heart skips a beat. You,
Bm
E7♭9
A
C#m
4fr
Bm
E7♭9
I real - ly real - ly need you but yet you play me for a

A
C♯m
Bm
E7♭9
To Coda
A
fool.
Why do you do me like you do, do, do,
E7
A
C♯m
Bm
E7
do? Yeah, aah, ahh,
A
C♯m
Bm
E7
A
C♯m
ahh, ahh, aah, ahh,
Bm
E7
A
D.S. al Coda
aah.
Well,

CODA
A
C♯m
Bm
E7♭9
A
do?
Why do you do me like you do,
why,
E7
A
C♯m
Bm
E7
why? Yeah,
ahh,
ahh,
A
C♯m
Bm
E7
A
C♯m
ahh,
ahh,
ahh,
ahh,
Bm
E7
A
C♯m
Bm
E
Optional Ending
A
Repeat and Fade
ahh.

GREECE

Words and Music by
GEORGE HARRISON

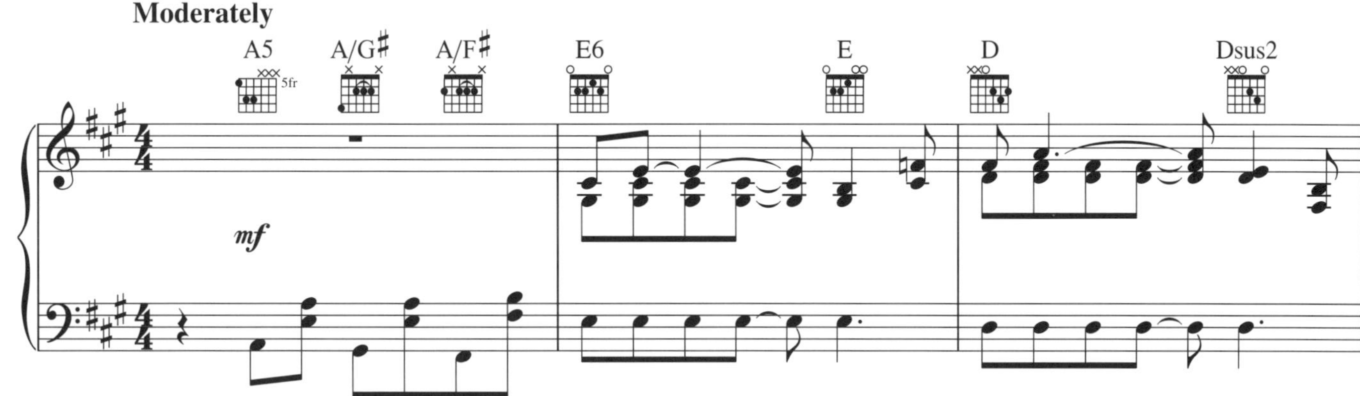

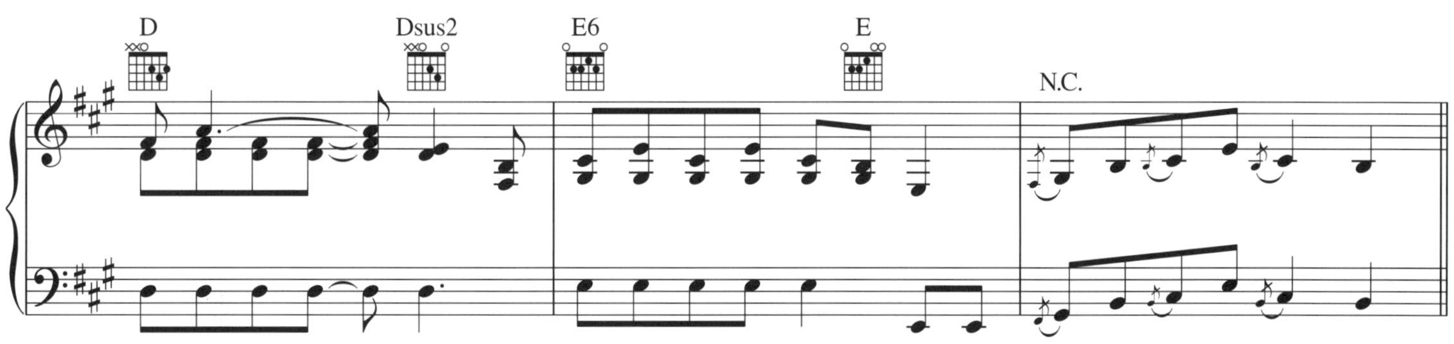

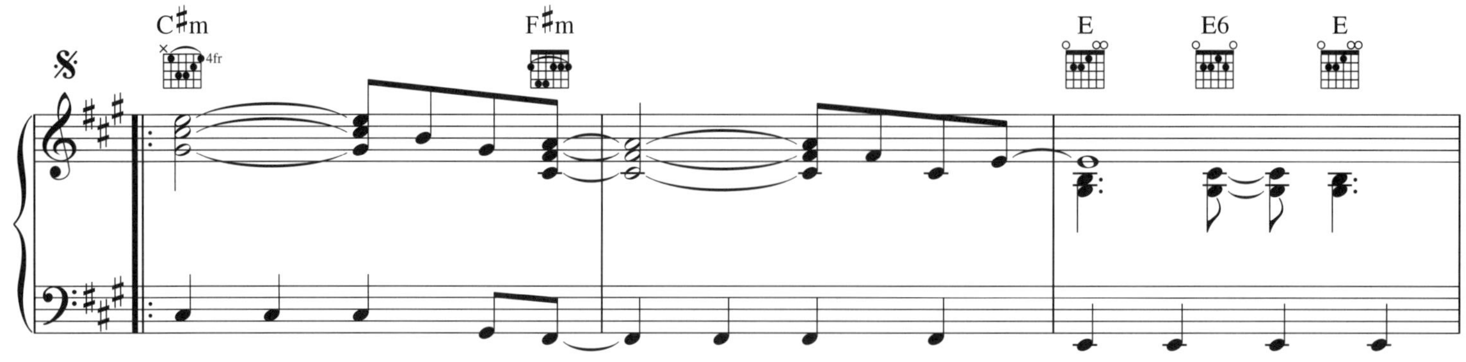
C♯m
4fr
F♯m
E
E6
E

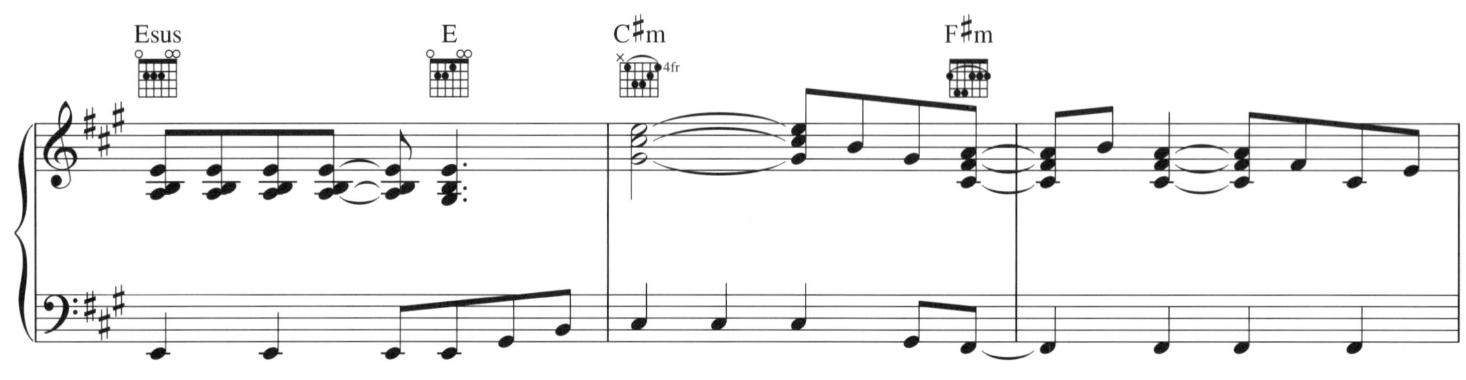
Esus
E
C♯m
4fr
F♯m

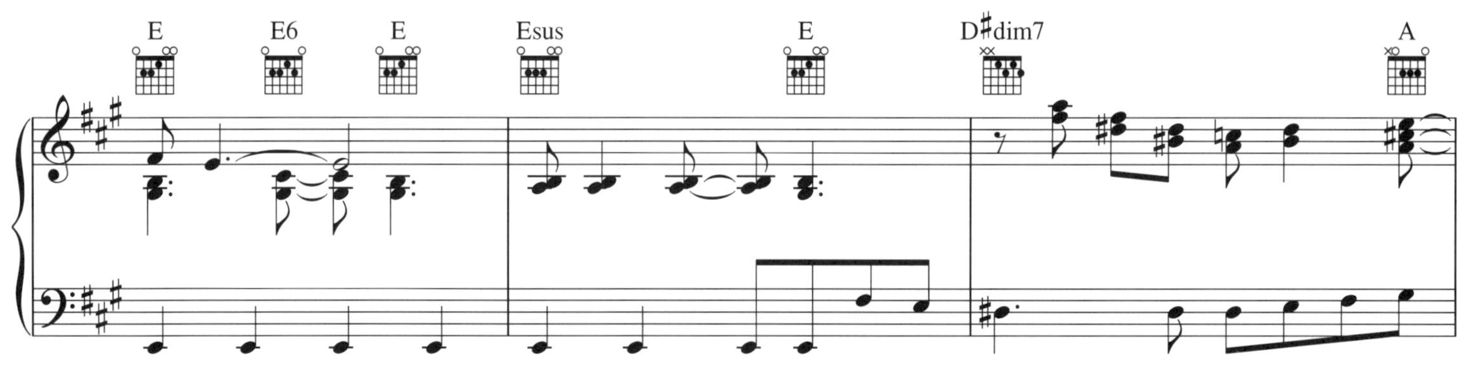
E
E6
E
Esus
E
D♯dim7
A

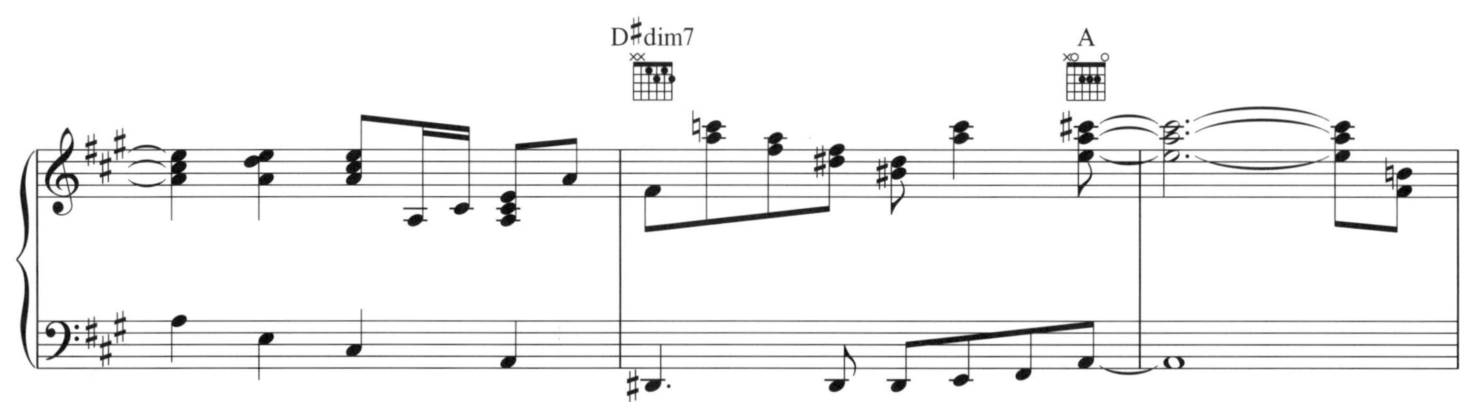
D♯dim7
A

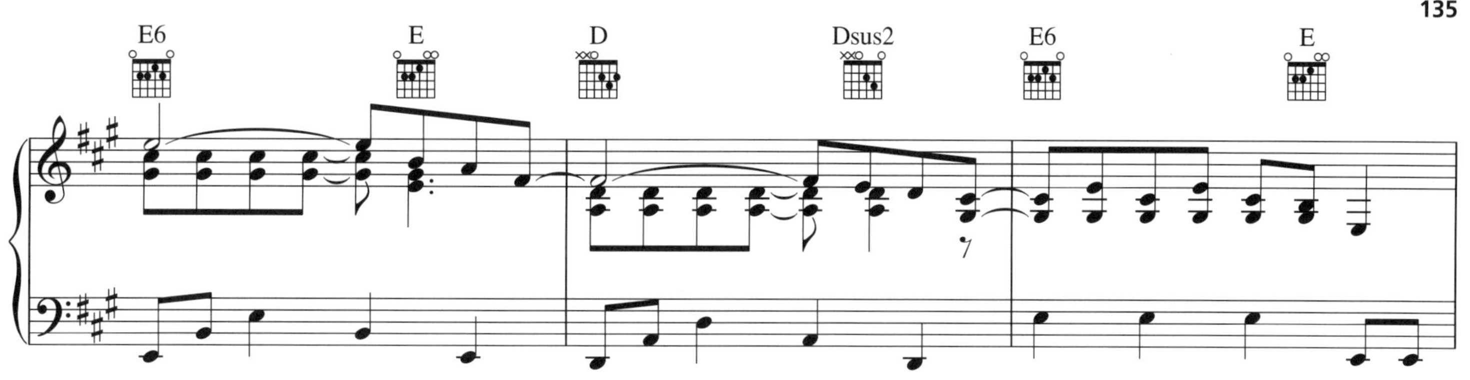
E6
E
D
Dsus2
E6
E

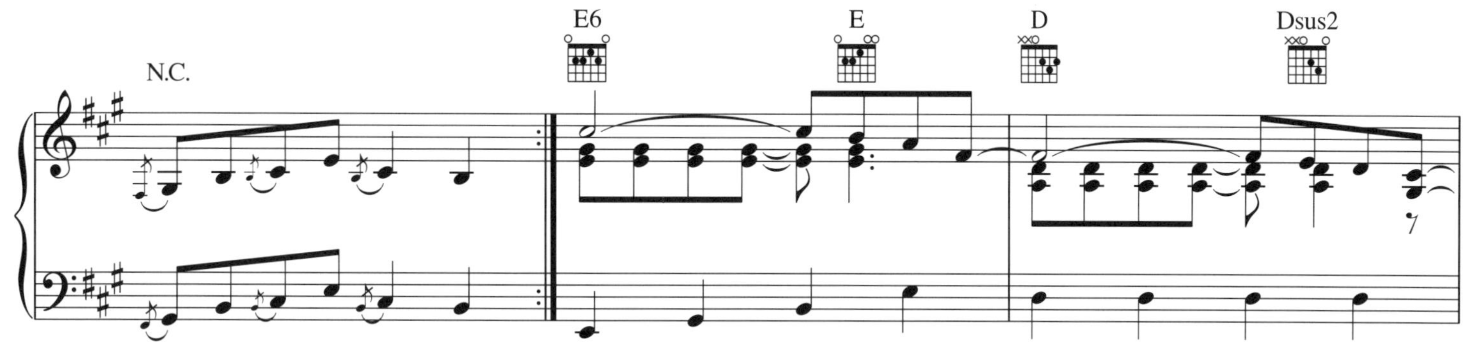
N.C.
E6
E
D
Dsus2

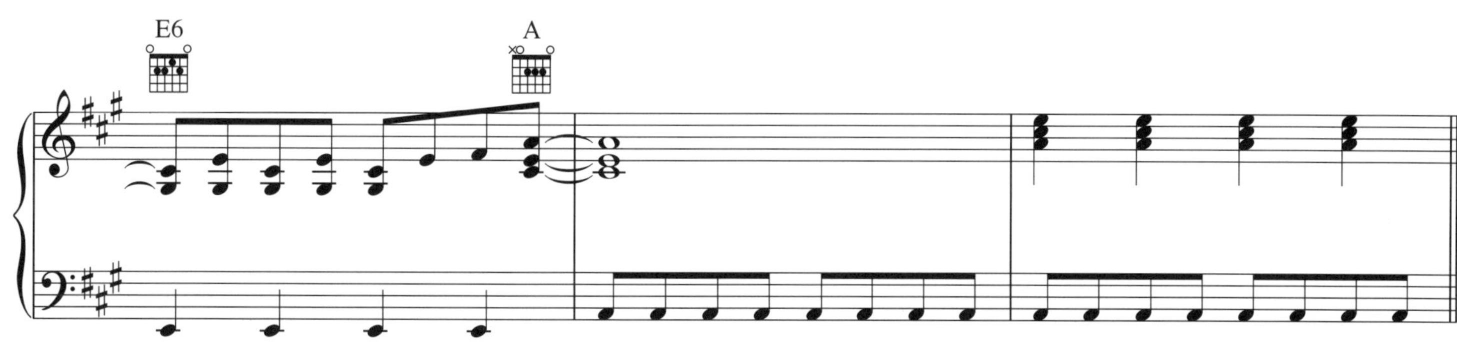
E6
A

F
A
Wel - come to Slo - via. Not past Ar - men - ia. Wel - come to Lourdes and lay.
Home-made A - then - a, hand - ed on Pla - to. Hole in my So - cra - tes.

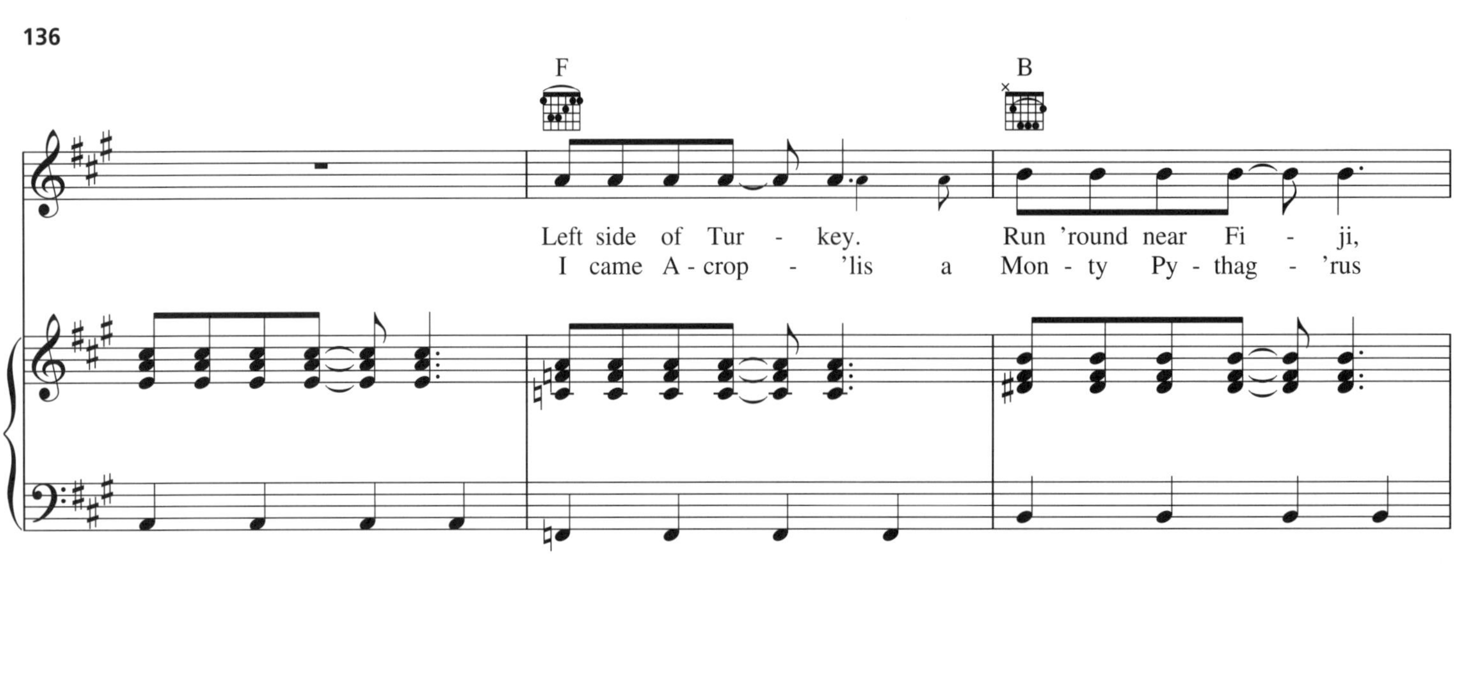
F
B
Left side of Tur - key. Run 'round near Fi - ji,
I came A - crop - 'lis a Mon - ty Py - thag - 'rus

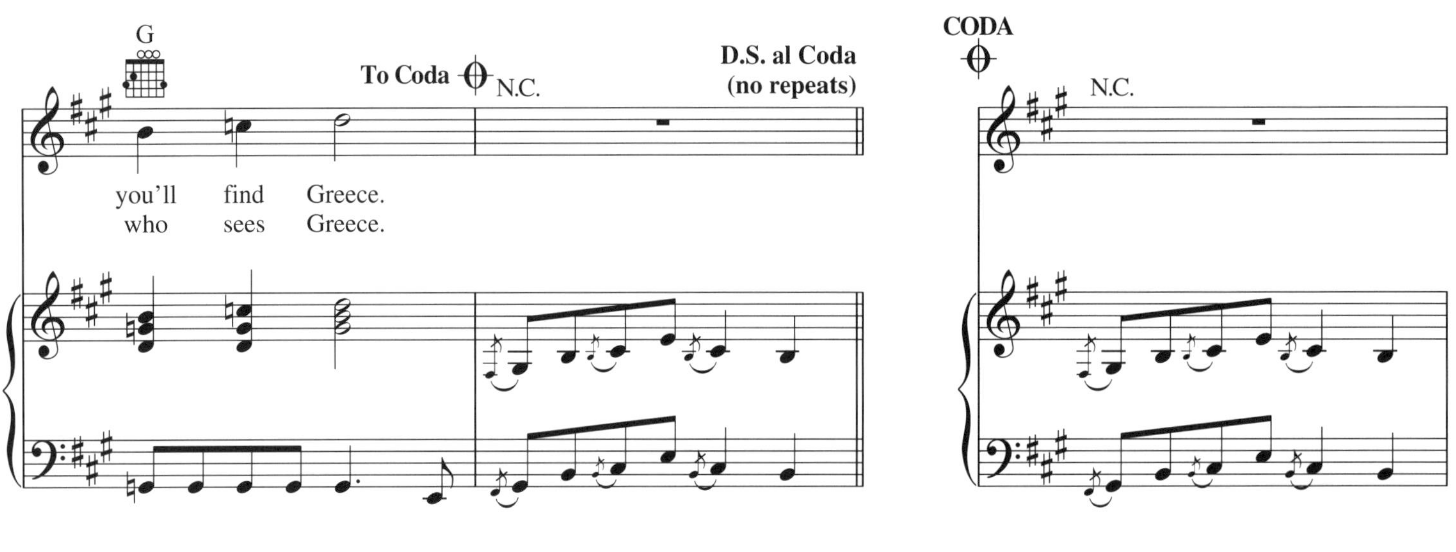
G
To Coda
N.C.
D.S. al Coda
(no repeats)
CODA
N.C.
you'll find Greece.
who sees Greece.

C♯m
4fr
F♯m
E
Esus
E

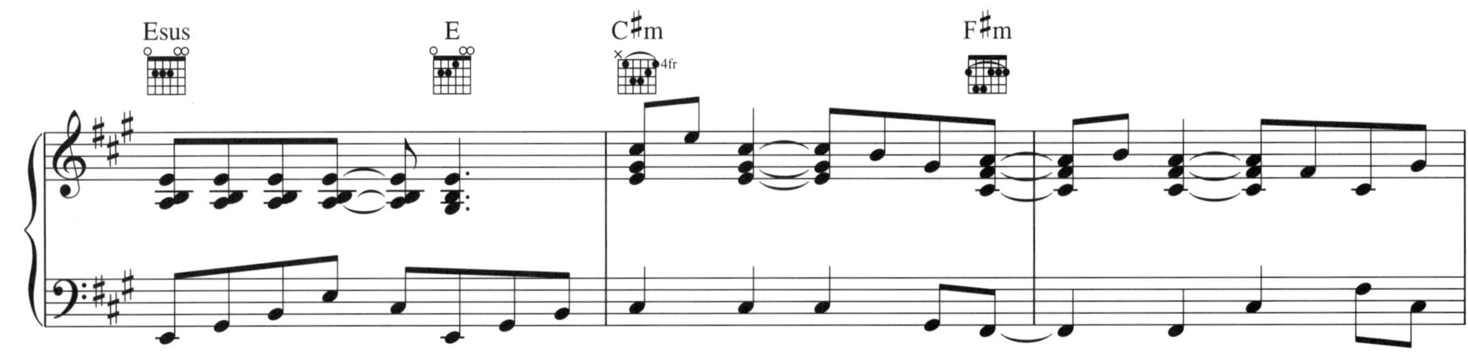
Esus
E
C♯m
4fr
F♯m

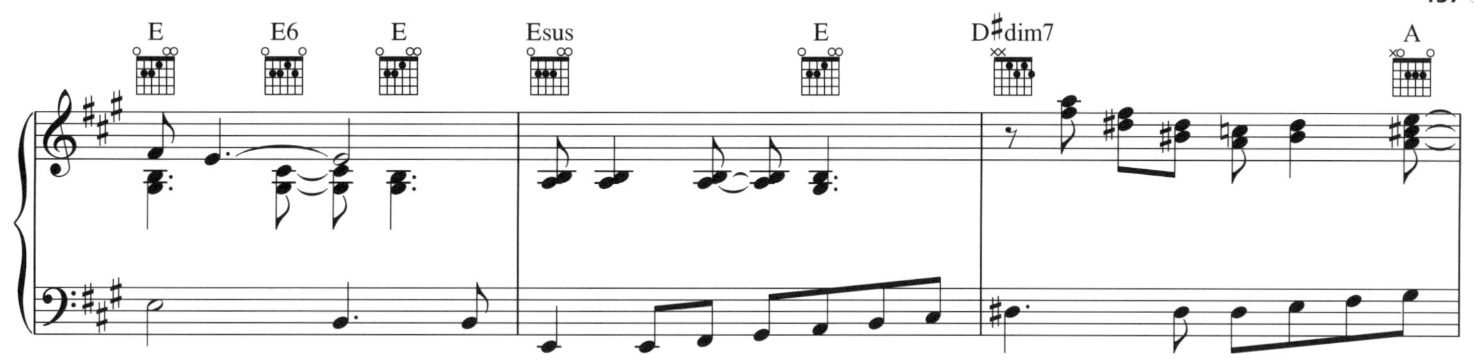
E
E6
E
Esus
E
D♯dim7
A

D♯dim7
A

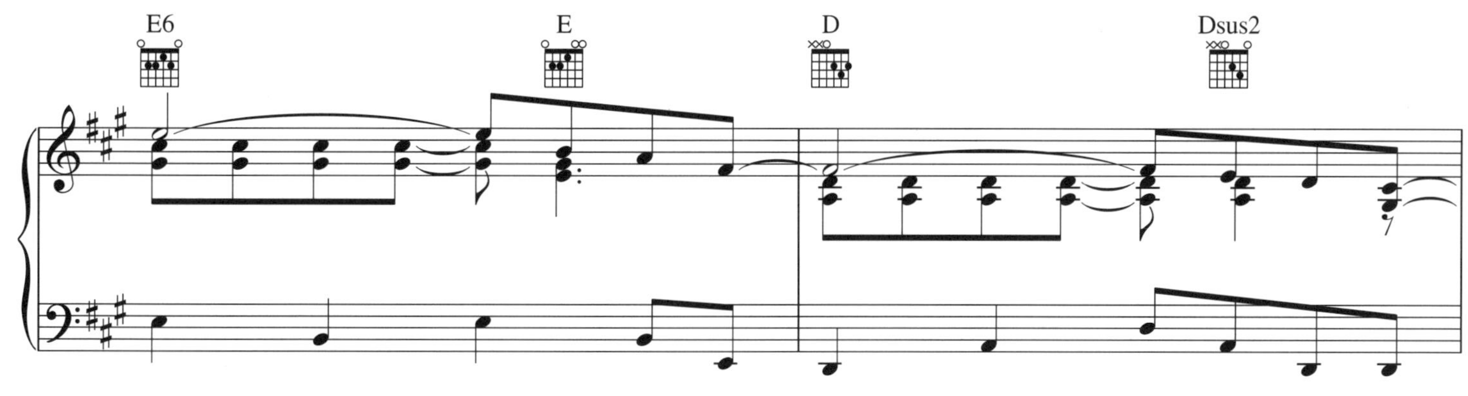
E6
E
D
Dsus2

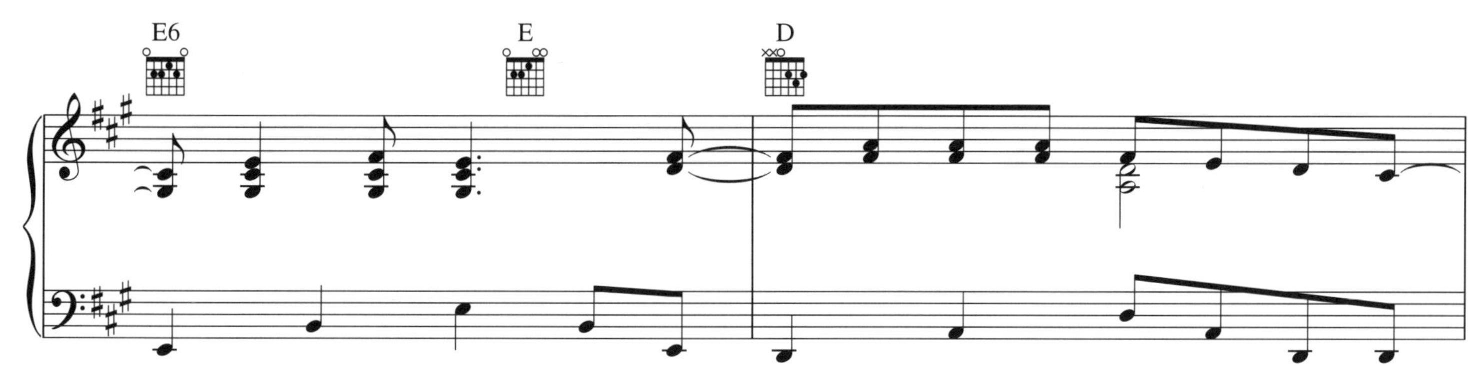
E6
E
D

E
D
E6
E

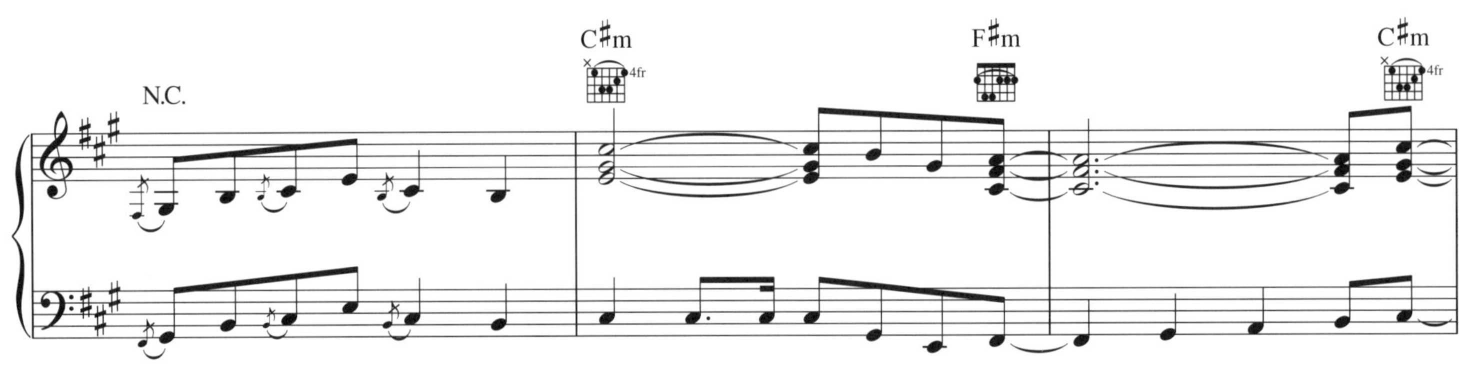
N.C.
C♯m
4fr
F♯m
C♯m
4fr

F♯m
C♯m
4fr
F♯m

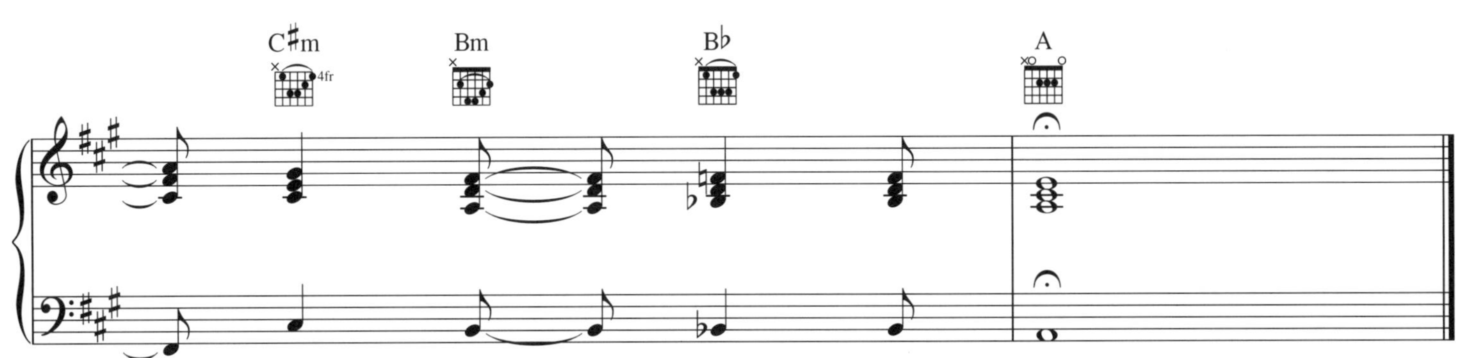
C♯m
4fr
Bm
B♭
A

HERE COMES THE MOON

Words and Music by
GEORGE HARRISON

C7
D7sus4
G
Bm7
__ it is, and __ here it comes. __
__ it does, and __ here it comes. __
__ it is, and __ here it comes. __
__ it is, and __ here it comes. __
Here comes the moon, the moon, __ the moon,
Em7
G7/D
C
A
the moon, the moon, the moon. ____
Here comes the moon, the moon, __ the moon,
A7
1.
D
the moon, the moon, the moon. ____
Oh, yeah. ____
2.
Here comes the moon, the moon, __ the moon,

Em7
G7/D
C
A7
To Coda
D
the moon, the moon.
Oh, yeah.
G
God's_ gift I
Am7
D7
G
see that's mov - ing up there in-to the_ night.
Though_ dark,
Am7
D7
G
D.S. (with repeats) al Coda
the mir-ror in the sky_ re - flects_ us our_ light.

Coda
G
Bm7
Em7
G7/D
Here comes the moon, the moon, the moon, the moon, the moon, the moon.
C
A7
D
Oh, yeah.
D
1. 2.
G
A
(mf)
f
3.
G
Repeat and fade
G
Repeat and fade

HONG KONG BLUES

Words and Music by
HOAGY CARMICHAEL

C♯m
4fr.
C♯m7
4fr.
Kong. He got twen - ty years' priv - i - lege tak - en a -
C♯m6
3fr.
Amaj7/C♯
2 fr.
To Coda
G♯7+5
4fr.
way from him when he kicked old Bud - dha's gong.
C♯m
4fr.
B
E
Now he's pop-pin' the pi-an-o just to raise the price of a
C♯m
4fr.
Amaj7
G♯7
4fr.
tick - et to the land of the free. Well, he

E
says his home's in Fris - co where they send the rice, but it's
B7
E
G♯7
4fr.
real - ly in Ten - nes - see.
That's why he
C♯m
4fr.
G♯
4fr.
C♯m
4fr.
says:
"I need some-one to
3
G♯7
4fr.
C♯m
4fr.
C♯m/B
love me. I need some- bod - y to car - ry me home

Amaj7
G♯7
4fr.
C♯m
4fr.
E6
A
B
E
to San- Fran-cis-co and bur-y my bod-y there.
G♯7
4fr.
C♯m
4fr.
I need some-one to lend me a
C♯m/B
fif - ty - dol - lar bill, and then I'll leave
A7
G♯7
4fr.
C♯m
4fr.
E6
A
B
Hong Kong be - hind me for hap-pi-ness once a -

E A E A

gain. Won't some-bod - y be - lieve

A#o7 E E7

I've a yen to see that bay a - gain?

A A#o7

Ev - 'ry time I try to leave, sweet

E G#7 4fr. C#m 4fr.

o- pi - um won't let me fly a - way. I need some-one to

G#7
4fr.
love me. I need some - bod - y to
C#m
C#m/B
A7
car - ry me home to San Fran-
E
A
B
cis - co and bur - y my bod - y there."
D.C. al Coda
Coda
kicked old Bud-dha's gong.

IF YOU BELIEVE

Words and Music by GEORGE HARRISON
and GARY WRIGHT

Fm
G
C/G
G7
new day may bring to you.
the holes they dig for you.
C
C7
F
Or take each day as it goes on; wake up to the love
Get up; you have all your needs. Pray give up, and it all
Fm
G
C/G
G7
that flows on a - round you.
re - cedes a - way from you.
If you be - lieve,
C
F
if you be - lieve in you,

Fm
G
C
ev - 'ry-thing_ you thought_ is pos - si - ble. If you be-lieve,_
F
Fm
if you be-lieve_ in me,_
all your love's_ re - flect - ed back_
1.
G
C
C7
F
when you be - lieve._
Fm
G
2.
G
D. S. 𝄋 and fade
_ to you. If you be - lieve,_

JUST FOR TODAY

Words and Music by
GEORGE HARRISON

Am
Em
B
Em
night, I could feel not sad and lone-ly, not
Dm
C
Em/B
Am
E
be my own life's prob-lem, just for one night.
G
C
Am
If just
Just
for to-day, I could
Em
B
Em
Dm
try to live through this day on-ly, not deal with all life's

C
Em/B
Am
E
G
N.C.
prob - lems,
just for to - day.
Just for to -
Am
Em
B
day.
Instrumental solo
Em
Dm
C
Em/B
Am
E
1
G
2
G
C
Solo ends
If

IT'S WHAT YOU VALUE

Words and Music by
GEORGE HARRISON

D
B
E7
Some - one's driv - ing a Four - Fif - ty, and his friends_ are
Some - one's driv - ing a six - wheel - er; seems the world_ is
D
A
D
B
so_ wild._ They're still in their stick shift - ies;
all_ blurred._ Knows he's in a show steal - er
E7
D
A
G7
they feel_ they have much_ more_ style,_ but I've found:_
with a sound_ that's un - com - pared,_ and I've found:_
D
C
G7
It's all up_ to_ what_ you val - ue_ down_

D
C
F
Am
to where you are.
It all swings on the pain you've gone through
B♭
A7
D
C
G7
get-ting where you are.
It's all up to what you val - ue in
D
C
F
Am
your mo-tor-car.
It all rests on what it's cost you
B♭
A7
To Coda
Bm9
E7
A
get-ting where you are; it's what you val - ue.

D
B
E7
D
A
D
B
E7
D
A
D.S. 𝄋 al Coda
Coda
Bm9
E7
Bm9
E7
A
ue.
D
B
E7
D
A

LEARNING HOW TO LOVE YOU

Words and Music by
GEORGE HARRISON

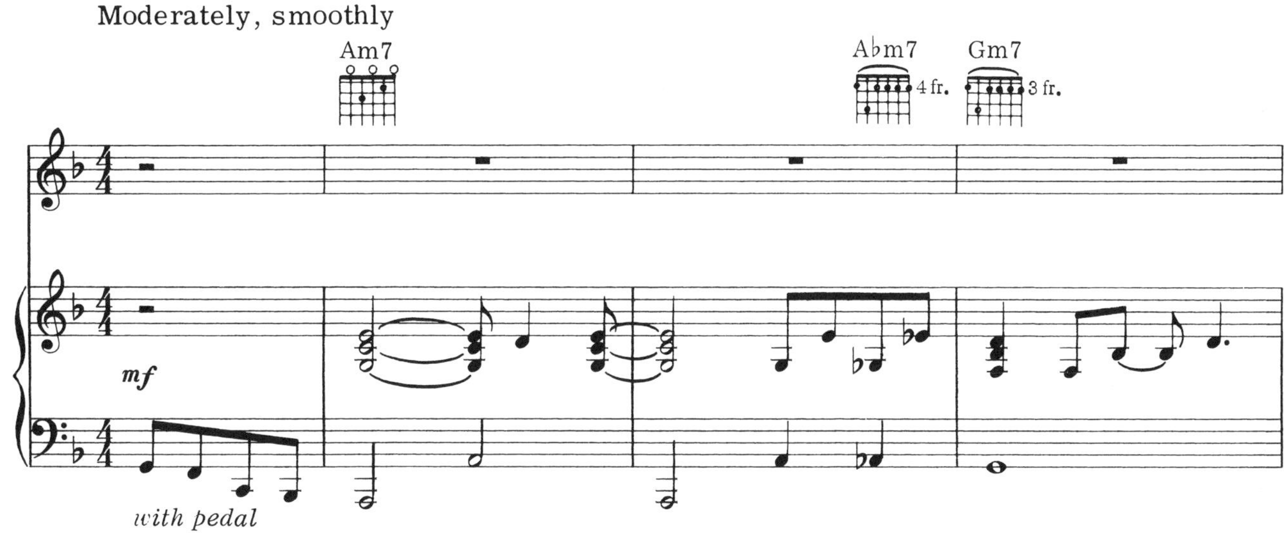

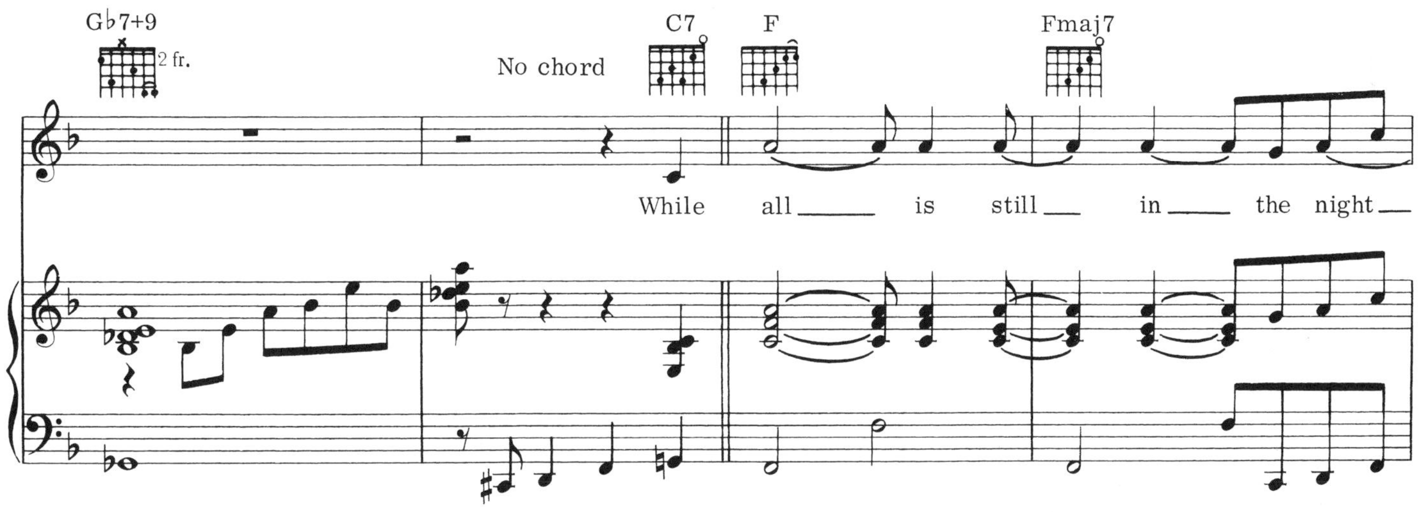

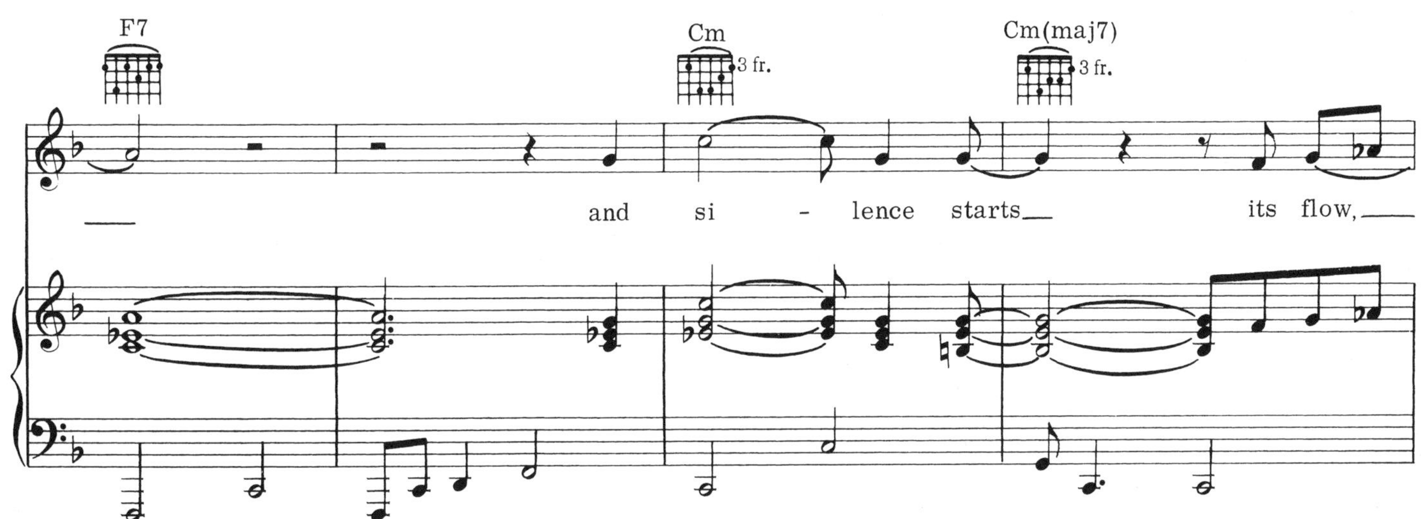

Cm7
3 fr.
F7
be - come or dis - be - lieve
Bb
Am
Am7
me.
Left a - lone with my heart, I'm
Gm7
3 fr.
Gb7+9
2 fr.
learn - ing how to love you.
While
F
Fmaj7
F7
wait - ing on the Light, how

Cm
3 fr.
Cm(maj7)
3 fr.
Cm7
3 fr.
pa - tience learned to grow. En -
F7
F7-9
B♭
deav - or could re - lieve me.
Am
Am7
A♭m7
4 fr.
Left a - lone with my heart, I
Gm7
3 fr.
G♭7+9
2 fr.
know that I can love you.

Gm9
3 fr.
Gm
3 fr.
Gm9
3 fr.
Gm
3 fr.
Love you like you may have nev - er {been, seen,}
Ebmaj9
5 fr.
Eb
6 fr.
Ebmaj9
5 fr.
Eb
6 fr.
move you more ways than you have {seen, been,} to a point
Cm7
3 fr.
in the time where we see so much more than the ground
Ebm7
6 fr.
Gm7
3 fr.
that we touch with each step so un -

C9
C7
F
Fmaj7
sure. As tear - drops cloud the sight,
F7
Cm
3 fr.
Cm(maj7)
3 fr.
your eyes may nev - er know.
Cm7
3 fr.
F7
F7-9
No truth could ev - er
Bb
To Coda
Am
Am7
fear me. Left a - lone with my heart,

Gm7
3 fr.
G♭7+9
2 fr.
D.S. 𝄋 al Coda 𝄌
learn - ing how to love you.
Coda
Am
And left a - lone with my heart,
Am7
Gm7
3 fr.
G♭7+9
2 fr.
learn - ing how to love you.
N.C.
B7
B♭maj7
Fmaj7

LIFE ITSELF

Words and Music by
GEORGE HARRISON

Moderately

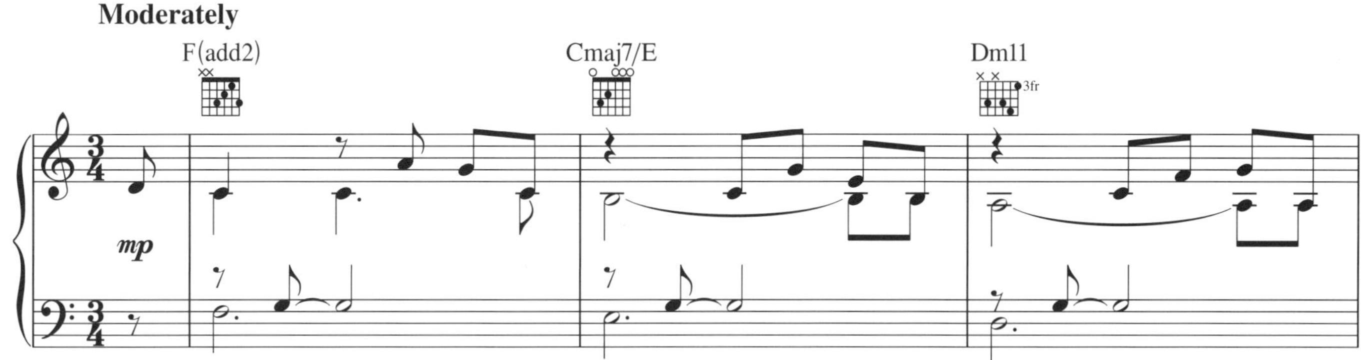

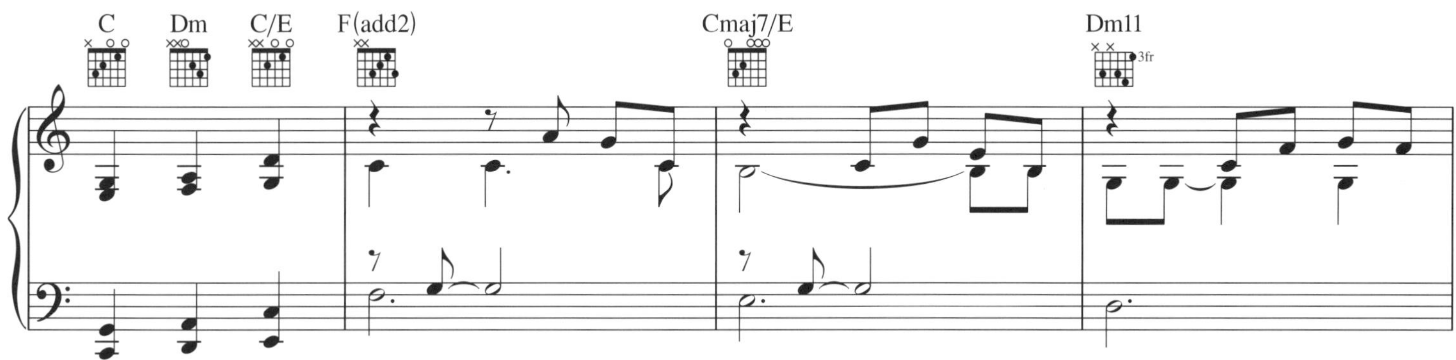

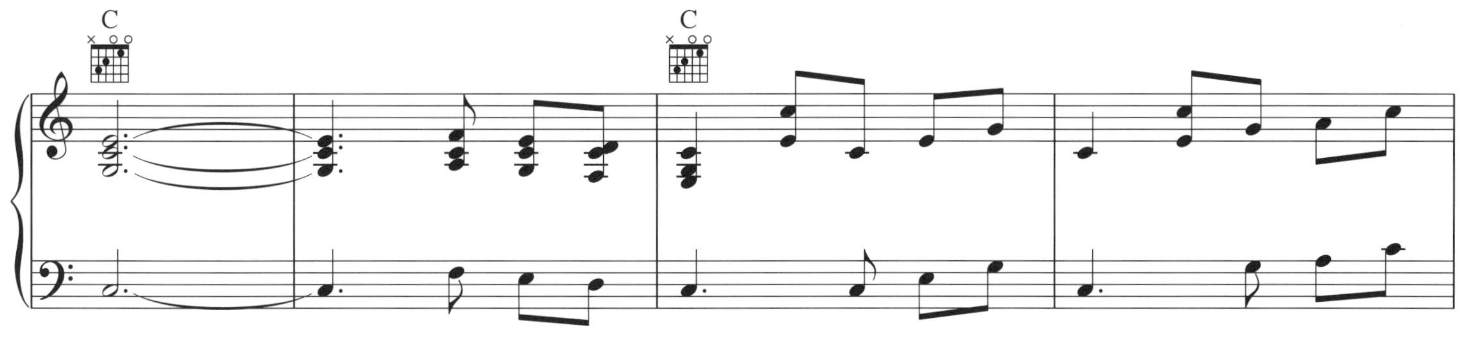

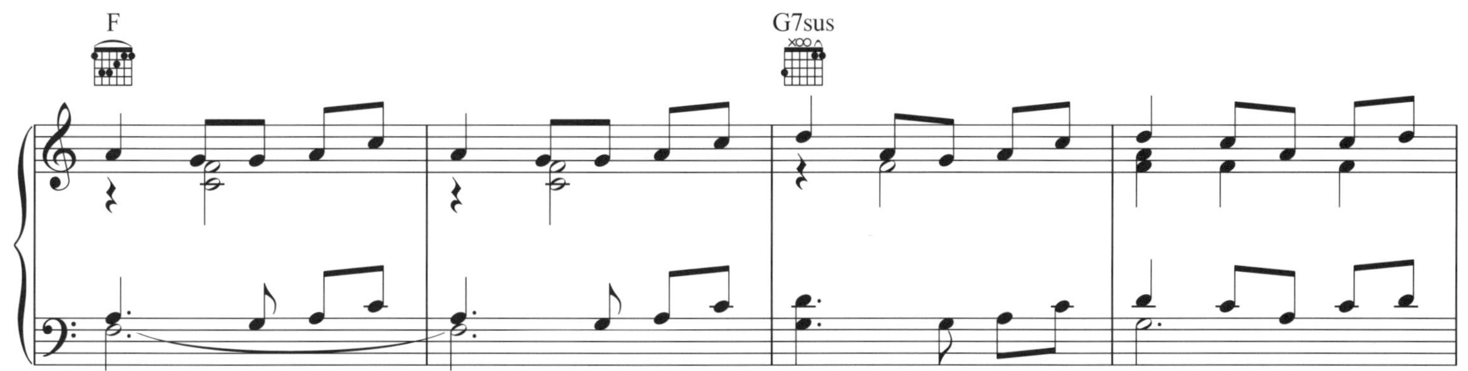

C
You are the
C
F
One. You are my love. You send the rain and bring the sun. You stand a -
One. Guitar solo ad lib.
G7sus
lone and speak the truth. You are the breath of life it - self, oh yes you are. You are the
C
F
One. You're in my dream. I hold you there in high es - teem. I need you

G7sus
more, each step I take. You are the love in life it-self, oh yes you are. You are the
C
G
One. You are the one that I'd die for and you're
(2.) Solo ends They call you Christ, Vish-nu, Budd - ha, Je-
F
C
G
all that is real. You are the es-sence of that
ho-vah, Our Lord. You are Go - vin-dam, Bis-mil - lah,
F
G
which we taste, touch and feel.
Cre - at - or of all.
You are the

C
F
One, no mat - ter what. You are the real love that I've got. You are my
G7sus
To Coda
friend, and when life's through, you are the light in death it - self, oh yes you are.
D.S. al Coda
CODA
You are the
C
yes you are. You are the One. You are my
F
G7sus
love. You send the rain and bring the sun. You stand a - lone. You speak the

truth. You are the breath of life it - self, oh yes you are. The breath of
life it - self, oh yes you are.
C
F
G7sus
Repeat and Fade
Optional Ending
C

LOVE COMES TO EVERYONE

Words and Music by
GEORGE HARRISON

E7
C♯m7
4 fr.
F♯m7
Bm7
y way out at all.
er rains, but it pours.
Still it on - ly takes time till love
D/E
E7
A
1.
2.
comes to ev - 'ry-one.
For
A
Dmaj7
A
E
D
There in your heart,
some - thing that's nev - er chang-
C♯m7
4fr.
A
Dmaj7
ing,
al - ways a part of

A
E
D
C♯m7
4fr.
Bm7
some - thing that's nev - er ag - ing. That's in your heart.
C♯m7
4 fr.
F♯m7
Bm7
It's so true, it can hap-pen to you all.
D/E
E7
C♯m7
4 fr.
F♯m7
There; knock and it will o - pen wide, and it on-
Bm7
D/E
E7
A
D. S. 𝄋 (instrumental) and fade
ly takes time till love comes to ev - 'ry-one.

MYSTICAL ONE

Words and Music by
GEORGE HARRISON

Cm F G Bm
- pi - er than a wil - low tree. Shine or rain, sit -
- ti - ful feel - ing in my soul. Sounds I've heard like
D G
- ting here by a stream. Mmm, there's noth - ing I'd rath - er feel
hum - ming - birds in a dream. Mmm, that mys - ti - cal one I knew
A Cm F
in this world. You and your sweet ser - en -
is re - turned. Lull - ing me with those rain -
G Bm D
- i - ty rock - ing me. Melt - ing my heart a - way.
- cloud eyes. Tak - ing me, melt - ing my heart a - way.

G
Em
B7
C
A
I am, yes I am.
I know what I feel.
You came in my life and made me more real.
I know what-ev-er we may have been

Cm
F
G
3fr
in past times has sort - ed the truth out from the rest.
Bm
D
G
Win or lose, I al - ways knew you'd be there. Mmm, you an -
A
Cm
3fr
- swer my deep - est prayer in a song. Sim -
- ti - cal one I knew is re - turned. Lull -
To Coda
F
G
Bm
D
- mer - ing slow hand flow - ing clear. Mov - ing me, melt -
- ing me with those rain - cloud eyes. Tak - ing me, melt -

G
- ing my heart a - way.
I
Em
B7
am, yes I am.
I know what I feel.
You came in my life,
C
A
made me more real.
D.S. al Coda
Mmm, that mys -
CODA
- ing my heart a - way.

G
Cm
3fr
F
G
Bm
D
Tak - ing me, melt - ing my heart a - way,
G
A
umm.
Cm
3fr
F
G

D
G
(Lead guitar ad lib. on repeat)

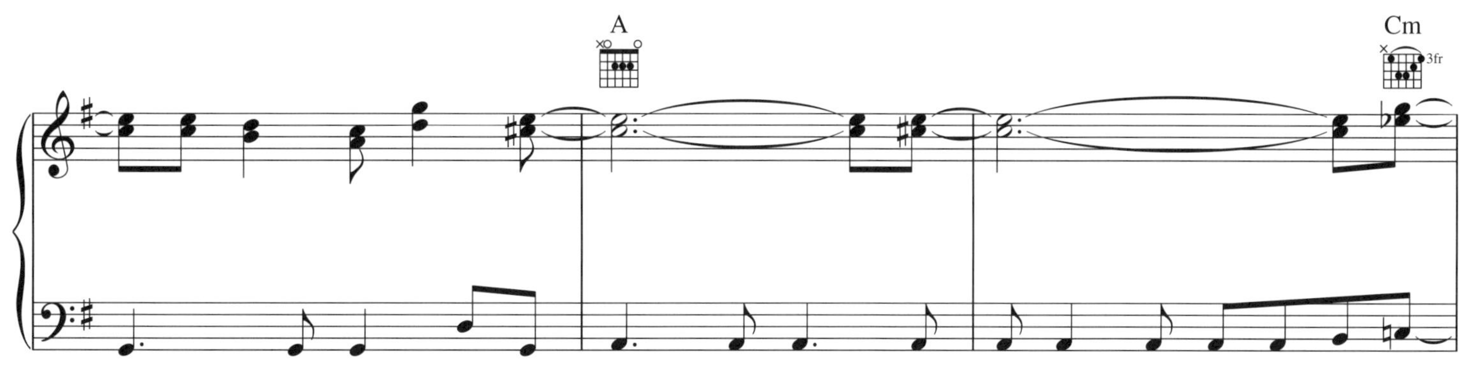
A
Cm
3fr

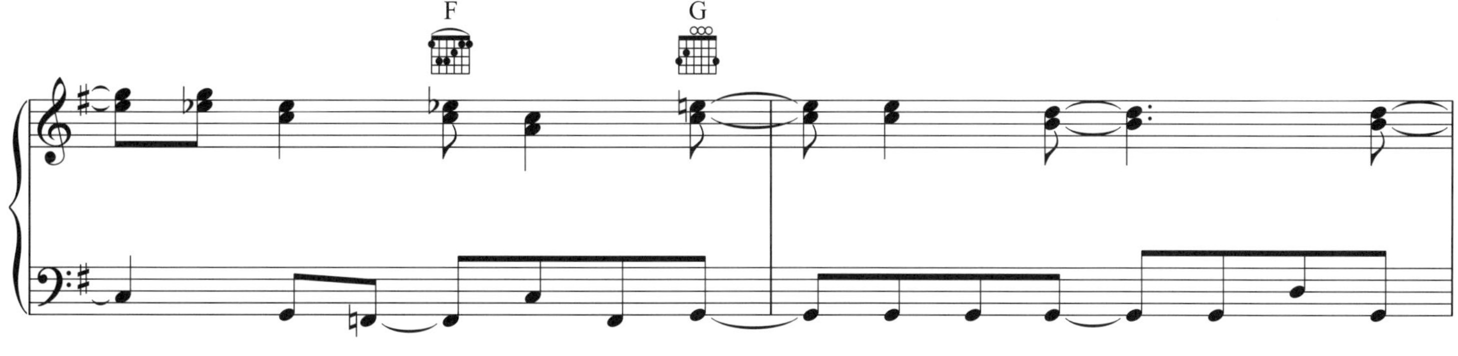
F
G

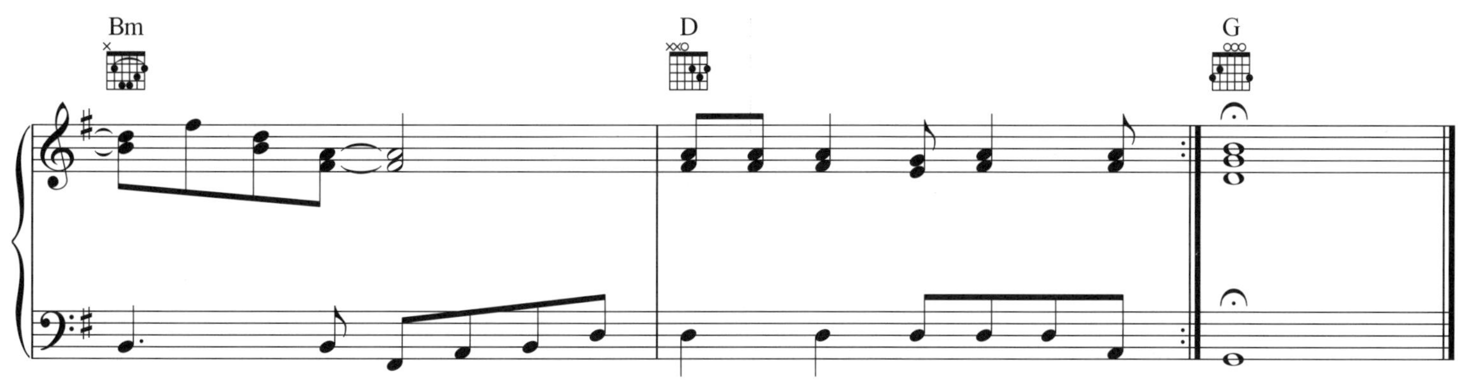
Bm
D
G

PURE SMOKEY

Words and Music by
GEORGE HARRISON

F♯m7
Em7
Bm7
F
C
G
F
C
(Smok - ey,
G
A7
D
Smok - ey,
ooh.)
(End solo)
Through-out my life -

F♯m7
- times I'd hes - i - tate.
Em7
Bm7
I'd feel some joy but be - fore I'd show my thanks
Gmaj9
it be - came too late.
D
F♯m7
But now all the way I want to find the time.

Em7
And stop to say I want to
Bm7
F
C
thank you Lord for giv - ing us each new day,
G
A7sus
D
think - ing back o - ver so
F♯m7
Em7
many - y years.
Love that's filled my

Bm7
ears. I want to thank you Lord for giv - ing us Pure
Gmaj9
D
Smok - ey. Ooh, and
F♯m7
an - y - one who hears that voice so free. He
Em7
Bm7
real - ly got a hold on me. And I thank you Lord for giv -

F
C
- ing us Pure Smok - ey, Pure
G
F
C
Smok - ey. Ooh, Smok - ey,
G
A7
Pure Smok - ey, ooh.
Dmaj7
F♯m7
(Guitar solo ad lib.)

Em7
Bm7
1
Gmaj9
2
F
C
G
A7sus
Dmaj7
F♯m7
He's sing - ing it so sweet - ly like no one else can do.
Em7
Al - ways try - ing some - thing new. And I

Bm7
Gmaj9
thank you all for giv - ing us Pure Smok - ey.
Dmaj7
And an - y - one who hears, hears that
F♯m7
Em7
voice so free. He real - ly got a hold on
Bm7
me. And I thank you Lord for giv - ing us Pure

F
C
G
A7
Dmaj7
Smok - ey,
Smok - ey,
ooh.
F♯m7
Em7
Bm7
Gmaj9
Dmaj7
Dmaj7♯11
Thank
you
Lord.

NOT GUILTY

Words and Music by
GEORGE HARRISON

Am
Am/G
F♯m7
B
Em
guilt - y,
and I'm not here for the rest.
I'm not
guilt - y.
No use hand-ing me a writ
while I'm
guilt - y
for lead-ing you a - stray
on the
B
G
Dm
try'n' to steal your vest.
Doo doo doo.
try'n' to do my bit.
Doo doo doo.
road to Man-da - lay.
E
I am not try - ing to be smart;
I on - ly want what I can get.
I don't ex - pect to take your heart;
I on - ly want what I can get.
I won't up - set the ap - ple cart;
I on - ly want what I can get.
Gsus
3 fr
Gm
3 fr
I'm real - ly
I'm real - ly
I'm real - ly

Em7
Em6
B7sus
4 fr
B7
To Coda
sor - ry for your ag - ing head, but like you heard me said, I'm not
sor - ry that you're un - der - fed, but like you heard me said, I'm not
sor - ry that you've been mis - led, but like you heard me said, I'm not
Am
Em7
Em6
Cmaj7/E
Em
guilt - y.
guilt - y.
Em7
Em6
Cmaj7/E
Em
Ooh, ooh,
Ooh, ooh,
Am
Am/G
F♯m7
B
Em
ooh.
ooh.

1
B
Em
2
B
Em
D.S. al Coda
Not
Not
CODA
Am
Em7
Em6
Cmaj7/E
Em
guilt - y.
Ooh, ooh,
Am
Am/G
F#m7
ooh.
Em7
Em6
Cmaj7/E
Em
Repeat and Fade
Ooh, ooh,

SAVE THE WORLD

Words and Music by
GEORGE HARRISON

F♯9
A
G♯7
4fr.
So far — we've seen this
but dog — food sales - men per -
So far — we've seen the
C♯m
4fr.
Em
F♯
plan-et's rape. How we've a - bused — it! —
sist un - kind - ly — to har - poon — it. —
big bus'-ness of ex - tinc-tion bleed — it. —
F♯+
B7
B°7
We've got to save the world. —
We've got to save the world. —
We've got to save the world. —

C♯m7-5/B B F♯

The Rus-sians have the big - gest share,_
The ar - ma-ment con-sor - ti - um,_
We're at the mer-cy of _ so few,_

B F♯7 E

with their long _ fin - gers ev -'ry - where._ And now they've bombs in out-
they're sell-ing _ us plu - to - ni - um._ Now you can make your own.
with e - vil _ hearts de - ter-mined to _ re-duce this plan - et in-

G♯7 4fr. E Em

er space _ with la-ser beams and a - tom - ic waste._
_ H - bomb _ right in the kitch-en with _ your mom._
to hell, _ then find a buy - er and make _ quick sale._

B7
Bo7
C♯m7-5/B
B
Rain for-ests chopped for pa -
Nu-clear power that costs
To end up - on a hap-
F♯
B
F♯7
per towels. One a - cre gone in ev - 'ry hour.
you more than an - y-thing you've known be - fore:
py note, like try -ing to make con - crete float,
E
G♯7
4fr.
E
Our birds and wild-life all de- stroyed to keep some mil - lion-aires
the half-wit's an-swer to a need for can-cer, death, de-struc-
is ver - y sim-ple, know - ing that God in your heart lives.

Em
B7
Bo7
C♯m7-5/B
— em - ployed. —
tion, greed. —
1.2.
F♯
F♯+
We've got to save the whale. -
We've got to save the world. -
3.
F♯
F♯+
We've got to save the world. -
B7
D♯m
A
C♯7
4fr.
Some-one else may want to use —
Do7
F♯9
A
it. —
It's time you knew -

G♯7
4fr.
C♯m
4fr.
how close we've come. We're gon-na lose
Em
F♯
it.
We got-ta
F♯+
save, we got-ta save, we got-ta save the
B7
B°7
C♯m7-5/B
B
world.

SEE YOURSELF

Words and Music by
GEORGE HARRISON

A
A7
D
F♯m/C♯
eas - i - er to crit - i - cize some - bod - y else than to see
eas - i - er to see the books up - on the shelf than to see
B7
1. A
2. A
your-self. (Oo.)
your-self. (Oo.)
It's
It's
A7
D
eas - i - er to hurt some - one and make them cry than it
E7
A
A7
is to dry their eyes. I got tired

D
Bm
A
F♯m7
of fool - ing 'round with oth - er peo - ple's lies, rath - er I'd
B7
E7
Bm7
E7
find some - one that's true. It's
A
Em7
eas - i - er to say you won't than it is to feel you can. It's
A
Em7
eas - i - er to drag your feet than it is to be a man. It's

A
A7
D
F♯m/C♯
eas - i - er to look at some - one else - 's wealth than to see
B7
A
A
your - self. (Oo.)
Em7
A
Em7
A
A7
It's eas - i - er to see the books up - on

D
F#m/C#
B7
the shelf than to see your-self.
(Oo.)
A
A7
It's eas-i-er to crit-i-cize some-bod-
D
F#m/C#
B7
y else than to see your-self.
A
(Oo.)
p

SHANGHAI SURPRISE

Words and Music by
GEORGE HARRISON

C
G
na. But I'm ready - y.
Female lead: You must be
C
G
C
cra - zy;
and you got no mon - ey;
G
C
G
and you're a li - ar.
and it seems like mad - ness.
Am7
D7
Am7
D7
Male lead: My straits are dire; from the, the wok in - to the fire.
Back streets so crowd - ed that no room to swing a cat.

Am7
D7
G
D/F#
Em
Bm/D
I'd like to trust you, but I've bro - ken my rick - shaw.
I'd like to know you, but you're act - ing so cool - ly.
Am7
D7
Am7
D7
Some - times there's no hop - in' in chas - ing o - pi - um. I'd
I'm find - ing I'm pur - sued by e - vil look - ing dudes. It's
Am7
D7
G
D/F#
Em
G/D
like to love you, but I'm not sure what's in your eyes.
get - ting hot for me, like to - fu when it deep fries.
Bm
Dm7
G7
Mm,
Oh,
Shang - hai Sur - prise.
Female lead: What - ev - er you're say - in',
But, ba - by, you look

Dm7 G7 Dm7 G7
I want it an - y - way - in'. Been hang - in' 'round like a
like an - y com - mon crook that's hang - in' 'round in those
C G/B Am Em/G Dm7 G7 Dm7 G7
kid at your back door. You could be kind - er, and show me A - sia Min - or.
real shad - y plac - es. While you as - sess me, why not try to im - press me?
Dm7 G7 C G/B Am C/G
I'll let you love me, let you see what's here in my eyes.
Step o - ver here, let me see what's there in your eyes.
Em A5
5fr
Shang - hai Sur - prise.

E5
1
C
G
2
You must be
Male lead: I
G5
3fr
don't un - der - stand how I got de - layed; I should be sail - ing to - day on the lin - er.
Was kicked in the ass on a dock at Yang - tse. It's no

C
way for a man to see Chi - na. But I'm read - y.
G
C
(Cra - zy.)
G
Female lead: You must be cra - zy; and you got no
C
(Mon - ey.)
G
C
mon - ey; but you're a try - er.
G
Am7
D7
Am7
D7
Male lead: My straits are dire; from the, the wok in - to the fire.

Am7
D7
G
D/F♯
Em
Bm/D
I'd like to meet you, but I've bro - ken my chop - sticks.
Some - times there's no hop - in' in chas - ing prom - is - es. I
wan - na love you, thought it could prove to be un - wise.
G/D
Bm
Shang - hai Sur - prise.
Dm7
G7
Female lead: What - ev - er you're say - in', I'm want - ing an - y way in.

Dm7
G7
C
G/B
Am
Em/G
Dm7
G7
Been hang - in' 'round for a ride on your rick - shaw. You may cor - rect me;
Dm7
G7
Dm7
G7
now that you've in - spect - ed me, come o - ver here, let me
C
G/B
Am
C/G
Em
feel you cut down to size. Oh, Shang - hai Sur - prise.
Am7
D7
Am7
D7
Male lead: My straits are dire from the, the wok in - to the fire.

Am7
D7
G
D/F♯
Em
Bm/D
I'd like to know you, but I'm not real - ly so - cial.
Am7
D7
Am7
D7
Some - times it's no joke; I can't cope with o - pi - um. I'd
Am7
D7
G
D/F♯
Em
G/D
Bm
like to love you, but I'm not sure what's in your eyes.
E5
Shang - hai Sur - prise.

Female lead: Shang - hai Sur - prise.
C5
3fr
Male lead: Shang - hai Sur - prise.

C
G
C
G
Female lead: And you got no
C
G
C
mon - ey;
but you're a try - er.
Repeat and Fade
G
Optional Ending
G
C

SOFT HEARTED HANA

Words and Music by
GEORGE HARRISON

E
once my eyes could see you.
my soft - heart - ed Han - a.
G
Bm
G
No soon-er had I ooped it down,
I felt so far off
She en-tered right in through my heart.
And now, al-though we're
A
D
F♯
from the ground I stood on.
miles a - part, I still feel her.

Bm
E
My legs seemed to me like high - rise build - ings.
She lives be - neath the cra - ter in___ the mead - ow.
G
Bm
My head was high up in the___ sky.___
She grows a - mong the fruit and___ grain.___
G
A
D
F♯
To Coda
My skin, the sun be - gan to fry___ like ba - con.
You can meet her af - ter heav - y rain___ has fall - en.

F#7
And then some-bod-y old ap-peared and asked had I come far, and
Sev-en na-ked na-tive girls swam sev-en sa-cred pools. Lone
Bm
had-n't they just seen me up on Ha-le-a-ka-la. I
Rang-er smok-in' doo-bies said, "You're break-in' all the rules. You'd
F#7
kept on bod-y surf-ing to pre-tend I had-n't heard. There was
bet-ter get your clothes on or else there'll be a row. If it
Bm
some-one there be-side me swim-ming like Rich-ard the Third. And I'm still
was-n't for my sun-stroke, I would take you on right now." And I'm still

E7
1.
2.
D.S. al Coda
smil - ing.
smil - ing.
Repeat and fade
Coda
Bm
Repeat and fade
E
G
Bm
G
A
D
F#

SOMEPLACE ELSE

Words and Music by
GEORGE HARRISON

C♯
D
Amaj7
G♯dim7
to me." And now I'm sad-dened like I've nev-er been, re-
me know that you'll be sad-dened like you've nev-er been, re-
Dm
Dm/F
Dm/A
E
A
gret-ting that we'll leave. And for a while, you could com-
gret-ting that we'll leave. And for a while, I could com-
E
C♯
F♯m
-fort me, and hold me for some time. I need you now,
-fort you, and hold you in my mind. I need you now.
B7
B♭maj7
A♯m7♭5
E
to be be-side me, while all my world is so un-ti-dy.
to be be-side me, while all my world is sad and cra-zy.

Amaj7
A
C♯
D
Lone - li - ness,
emp - ty fac - es.
Wish I
Amaj7
Ddim7
1 A
N.C.
could leave them all in some - place else.
A
Ddim7/A
A
N.C.
2 A
N.C.
I hope you
Instrumental solo
Amaj7
A
C♯
D
A/C♯
Ddim7

Dm/F
Dm/A
E
A
Solo ends
And for a while, you could com-
E
C♯
F♯m
fort me, and hold me for some time.
I need you now,
B7
B♭maj7
A♯m7♭5
E
to be beside me, while all my world is so un - ti - dy.
Amaj7
A
C♯
D
Lone - li - ness,
emp - ty fac - es.
Wish I

Amaj7
Ddim7
1
A
B7
E
could leave them all in some - place else.
2
A
N.C.
A
G♯dim7
A
N.C.
I think I'm
A
Ddim7
A
N.C.
gon - na leave them all in some - place else.
A
G♯dim7
A

SOFT TOUCH

Words and Music by
GEORGE HARRISON

D
A
D
A
You're a soft_ touch, ba - by,
like a snow-flake fall - ing.
As a cool_ wind blows_ me,
all the tree - tops whis - per
D
A
D
G/D
D
A
My whole heart_ is melt - ing.
to your soft_touch, ba - by.
D
A
D
As a warm_ sun ris - es,
in-to joy_ I'm sail -
As a new_ moon ris - es,
those i - deas_ of heav-
A
D
A
To Coda
ing
to your soft_ touch, ba - by.
en
fall in your soft touch, ba - by.

D
G/D
D
Bm
Bm/A
G♯m7-5
Gmaj7
Bm/F♯
Eyes that shine from depths of your soul,
Em7
Bm
Bm/A
fixed by their charm, take my con - trol.
Love so sweet as the
G♯m7-5
Gmaj7
Bm/F♯
Em7
o - cean is wide,
caught by your waves and drawn
Bm
to your side.
1. A
2. A
D.S. 𝄋 (lyric 1) al Coda

Coda
D
G/D
D
A
Repeat and fade
D
A
D
Repeat and fade
A
D
A
D
G/D
D
A

TEARDROPS

Words and Music by
GEORGE HARRISON

N. C.
D/A
A
G♯o
F♯m
E
tear - drops, do do do do do. So hard to take.
Bm7
E
D/A
A
G♯o
F♯m
I got a soak-ing with those tear - drops, do do do do
E
Bm7
E
To Coda
N.C.
D/A
A
do, and it feels like I have tak-en o-ver from the rain.
N. C.
D/A
A

A
E
E7
In the heart of the lone-ly man, in and out of love more of-ten than most oth-ers can.
In the eyes of the lone-ly one, ev-'ry-thing is cold and hope-less that he looks up-on.
F♯m
A/E
D
E
A
E
He walks the streets like the los-ers in some lov-er's game.
He needs a friend, a lov-er who can com-fort him.
D
E
And talks so sweet, but the news is al-ways
His deeds of-fend. He knows that he has

A
E
1.
D
E
2.
D
E
D.S.
al Coda
much the same.
brought on him.
Coda
N. C.
D/A
A
G♯o
F♯m
rain.
E
Bm7
E
Repeat
and fade
N.C.
D/A
A
Tear - drops, do
G♯o
F♯m
E
Bm7
E7
do do do do.

TEARS OF THE WORLD

Words and Music by
GEORGE HARRISON

B♭
A7
F
A7
Dm
A7
Dm
Stone - wall - ing, voic - es call - ing. Drown - ing in the tears of the world.
A7
Dm
B♭/D
Dm6
Dm7
Big bus' - ness call - ing ev - 'ry tune.
B♭
G7/B
F/C
A7
B♭
A7
Pol - lut - ing here and to the moon.
All na - tions, con -
F
A7
Dm
A7
Dm
- ser - va - tions. Drown - ing in the tears of the world.
But your life's

A7
E7
worth sav - ing.
been sleep - ing.
We should start be - hav - ing.
Has your heart been weep - ing
Bm
E7
Like the truth's been told by sav - iours through - out time.
o - ver all un - right - eous ac - tion in a world
G7
G9
9fr
Dm
B♭/D
Your down - fall, bring it on your - selves.
where bad jazz seems all they're lay - ing down?
All warn - ings fall
No use in turn -
Dm6
Dm7
B♭
G7/B
F/C
A7
up - on deaf ears.
ing your blind eye.
Their scorn com - pound - ing our worst fears.
You'll feel the heat as you fry.

To Coda
Bb
A7
F
A7
Dm
A7
Dm
No way out, hope - less souls shout. Drown - ing in the tears of the world.
Try your best. You'll find no rest. Drown - ing in the tears of the world.
A7
Dm
Bb/D
Dm6
Dm7
Bb
G7/B
C
A7
Bb
A7
F
A7
Dm
A7
Dm
Drown - ing in the tears of the world, tears of the world.

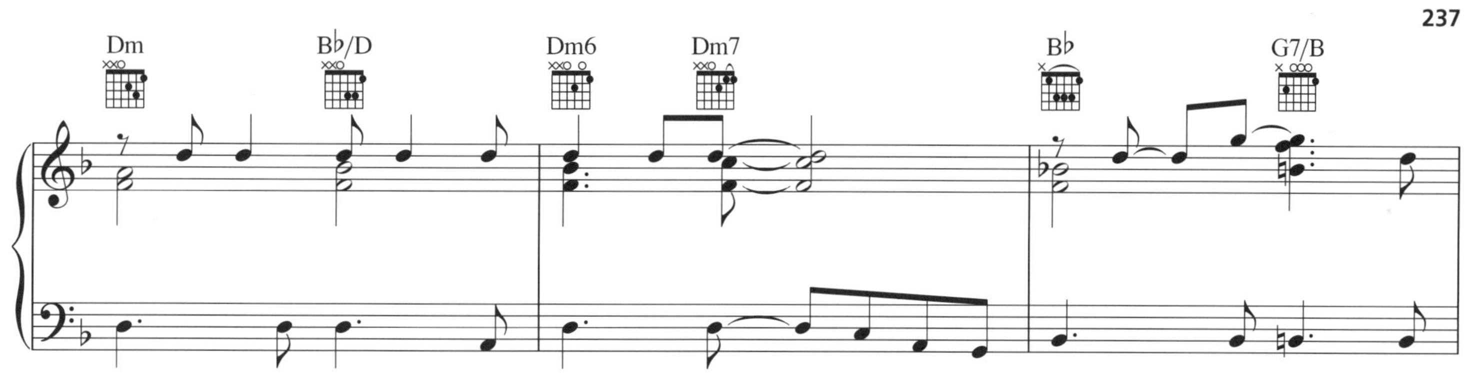
Dm
B♭/D
Dm6
Dm7
B♭
G7/B

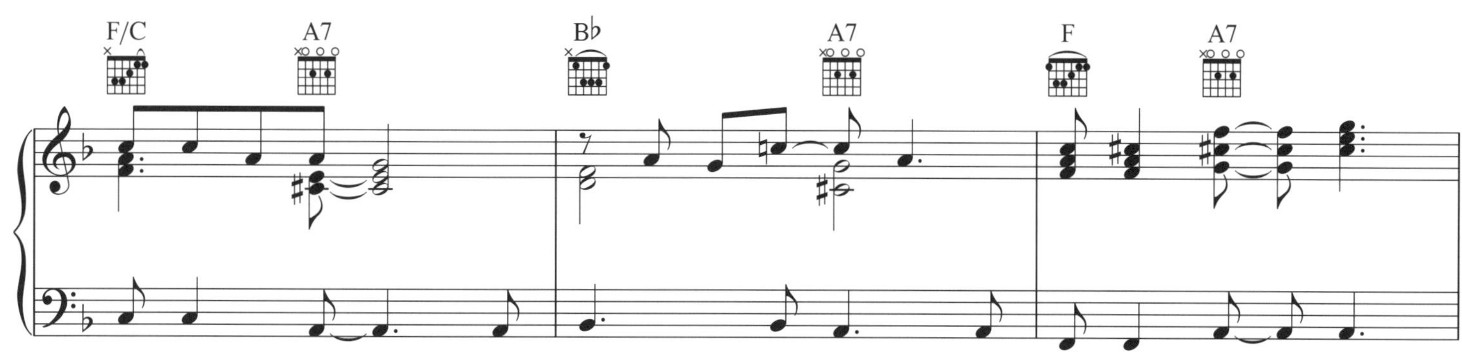
F/C
A7
B♭
A7
F
A7

Dm
A7
Dm
D.S. al Coda
Where's your love
CODA
Dm/C

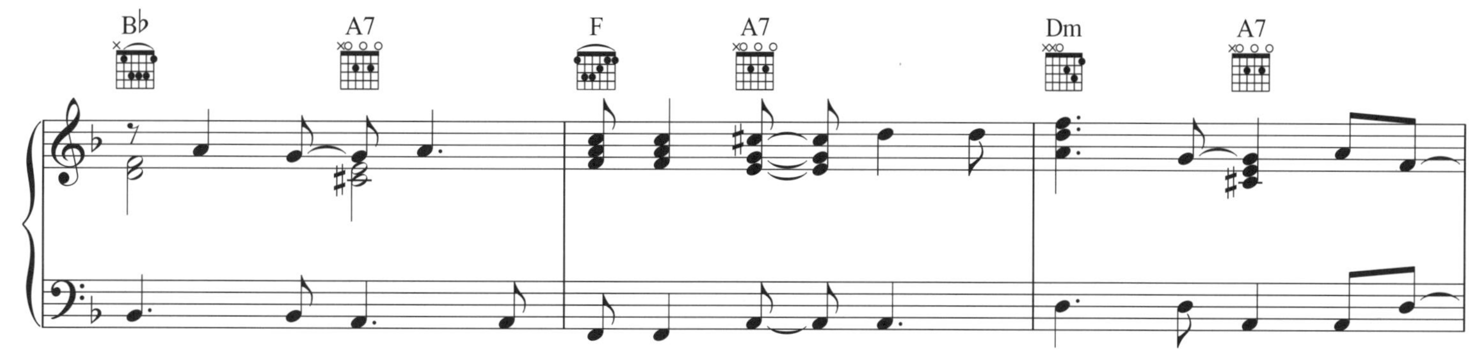
B♭
A7
F
A7
Dm
A7

Dm
Dm/C
B♭
A7
F
A7
It's a sure bet each pays his debt.
Dm
A7
Dm
A7
Drown - ing in the tears of the world.
Dm
(Ad lib. guitar solo)
A7
Dm
Repeat and Fade
Optional Ending

THAT WHICH I HAVE LOST

Words and Music by
GEORGE HARRISON

A
C
ta - tion, false - hood and mor - tal - i - ty which
break - ing. A flash. In - ward il - lu - mi -
to him. You're too bus - y fight - ing rev - o -
G
D
bar him the way back in - to the high - er world
na - tion en - riched his life more than an - y words can
lu - tions that keep you back down in the low - er world.
A
D
while his whole be - ing is be - wil - dered. He does
tell. He stood there, life re - newed fresh as
Your mir - rors of un - der - stand - ing, they need

A
C
not know. No law of ac-tion tak-ing
rain. Scales were fall-ing from his eyes a-
cleans-ing. Pol-ish a-way the dust of
G
ref-uge in-side him-self, and he's
gain, the bolts of his pris-on o-pen-ing. He's
de-sire be-fore pure light will re-
G(add A)
A7
D
say-ing: "I need some-one to show me,
say-ing: "I found some-one who showed me,
flect in them.. You need some-one to show you,

G7
il - lu - mine my con - scious - ness, _
il - lu - mined my con - scious - ness, _
il - lu - mine your con - scious - ness, _
E7
re - move _ the dark from in _ me _ and
re - moved the dark from in _ me _ and
re - move _ the dark from in _ you _ and
A7
give me _ that _ which I _ have lost." _
giv - en me that _ which I _ have lost." _
give you _ that _ which you _ have lost. _

D
G7
E7
D/A
A7
1. 2.
3.
As
You

THAT'S THE WAY IT GOES

Words and Music by
GEORGE HARRISON

G
D7
Seems he's lost some stocks and shares, stops and stares.
Sub - di - vide and deal it out, feel his clout.
C
G
C/G
He's a - fraid I know.
He can stoop so low.
1
That's the way it goes.

2
D7
G
C
There's an ac - tor who hopes to fit the bill, sees a shin - ing cit -

C
G
-y on a hill.
Step up close and
D7
C
see he's blind, wined and dined.
All he has is posed.
G
C/G
G
D7
G
And that's the way it goes.
D7
C
3

G
D7
G
There's a fire that
D7
C
burns a - way the lies man - i - fest - ing in the spir - i - tual eye.
G
D7
Though you won't un - der - stand the way I feel. You con - ceal

C
G
C/G
G
D7
all there is to know.
That's the way it goes.
G
D7
That's the way it goes.
G
D7
That's the way it goes.
G
D7

C
G
D7
That's the way it goes.
(Lead vocal and guitar ad lib. on repeat)
Repeat and Fade
Optional Ending

THAT'S WHAT IT TAKES

Words and Music by GEORGE HARRISON,
JEFF LYNNE and GARY WRIGHT

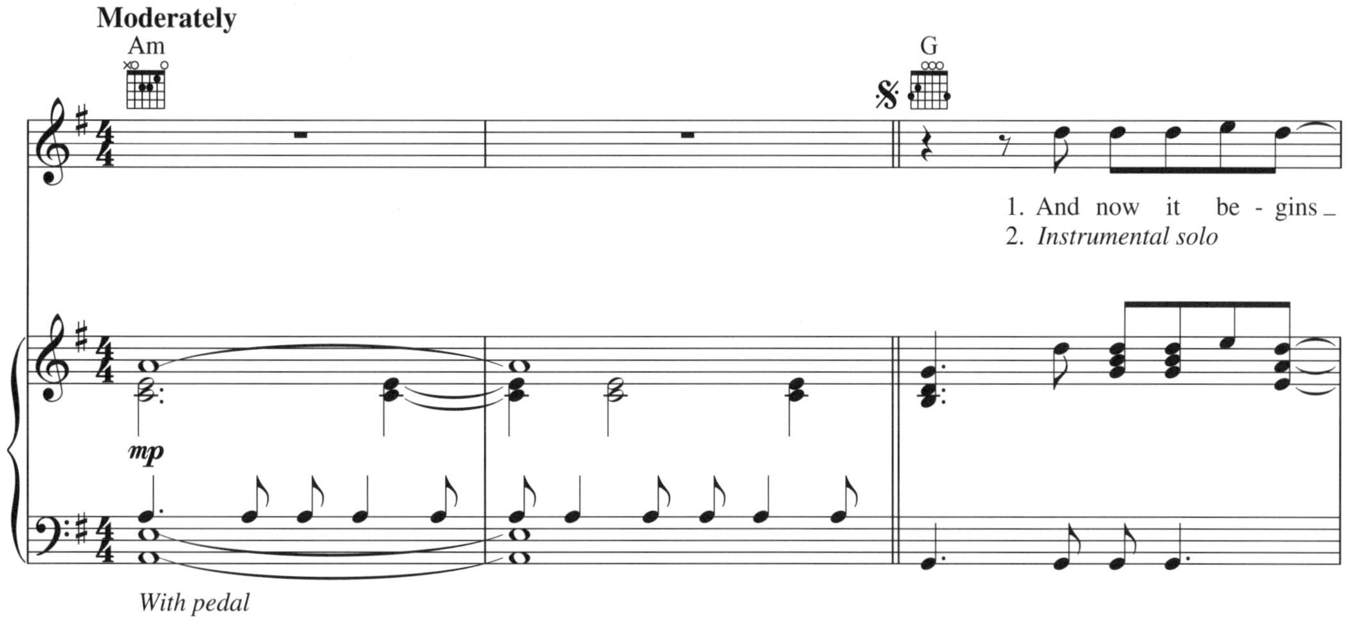

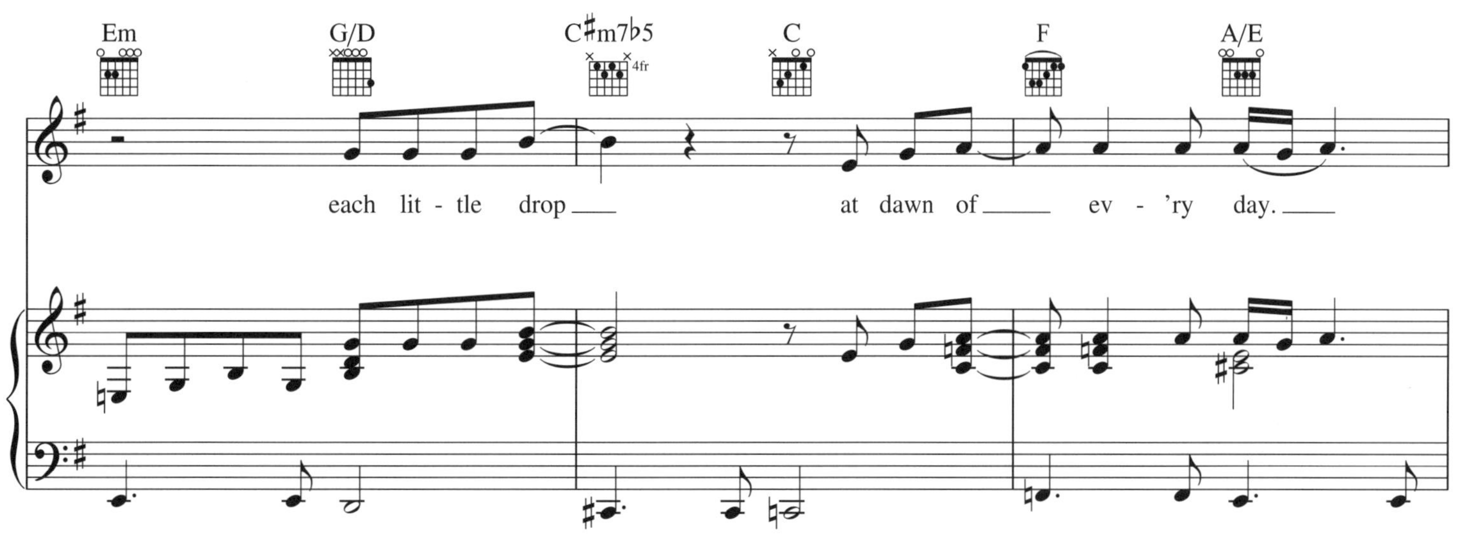

D
G
Asus
A
Solo ends
Your smile, it comes back to me;
And now that it's shin - ing through,
Am
Cm
3fr
Bm
Em
G/D
and what - ev - er you may say,
and you can see all this world,
don't let it stop;
don't let it stop;
C♯m7♭5
4fr
C
F
D
G
nev - er fade a - way.
nev - er fade a - way.
A♭/D♭
4fr
B♭m/E♭
A♭/B♭
4fr
E♭/F
As we got - ta get out in this world to - geth - er,
If we got - ta be in this life for - ev - er,

Eb/G
Ab
Ab/Bb
Ab/C
Ab/Db
Bbm/Eb
mm hm,
mm hm,
then we might as well stop
then we'd bet - ter be tak -
Ab/Bb
Eb/F
Eb/G
Ab
to make some chang - es.
- ing all the chanc - es.
Mm hm,
Mm hm,
Ab/Bb
C
F
G
mm hm.
mm hm.
If that's what it takes, then I
Instrumental solo
C/E
F
C/E
F
got - ta be strong; don't wan - na be wrong, if

G
Am
F
G
that's what it takes.
The clos - er I get in - to
C/E
F
C/E
F
that o - pen door,
I got - ta be sure,
if
1
G
Am
D.S.
that's what it takes.
2
G
Am
that's what it takes.
Instrumental solo
Repeat and Fade
G
Am
Optional Ending
G
Am

THIS IS LOVE

Words and Music by GEORGE HARRISON
and JEFF LYNNE

D
G
Em
melts the chill from our lives,
from way out of the blue,
A
G
A
helping us all to remember
making fools of ev'rybody
G
A
Bm(add4)
what we came here for.
who don't understand.
This is love,
Em7(add4)
5fr
Bm(add4)
Em7(add4)
5fr
this is la la la la love.
This is love,

Bm(add4)
Em7(add4)
5fr
Bm(add4)
this is la la la la love.
1
Em7(add4)
5fr
Lit - tle things
2
Em7(add4)
5fr
D
F#m/C#
D
F#m/C#
D
F#m/C#
(This is love.)
D
F#m/C#

3
Em7(add4)
5fr
D
(This is love.)
Solo ends
Since our prob - lems have been
G
Em
A
our own cre - a - tions,
D
G
Em
they al - so can be o - ver - come
A
G
A
when we use the pow'r pro - vid - ed,

G
A
Bm(add4)
free to ev - 'ry - one.
This is love,
Em7(add4)
5fr
Bm(add4)
Em7(add4)
5fr
this is la la la la love.
This is love,
Bm(add4)
Em7(add4)
5fr
Bm(add4)
this is la la la la love.
Em7(add4)
5fr
D
F♯m/C♯

D
F♯m/C♯
Bm(add4)
(This is love.)
Em7(add4)
5fr
Bm(add4)
Em7(add4)
5fr
This is la, la la la love. This is love,
Bm(add4)
Em7(add4)
5fr
Bm(add4)
this is la la la la love.
Repeat and Fade
Em7(add4)
5fr
This is love,
Optional Ending
Em7(add4)
5fr
D

THIS SONG

Words and Music by
GEORGE HARRISON

F♯m7
C♯m7
4 fr.
as I know don't in - fringe on an - y - one's cop -
er what may, my ex - pert tells me it's
or rare, may end up one more weight
F♯7
A/B
y - right, so this
o - kay. As this
to bear. But this
E
D
G♯m7
4 fr.
C♯7
4 fr.
song we'll let be. This song is in E;
song came to me quite un - know - ing - ly,
song could well be a rea - son to see

F♯m7
1. 2.
this song is for you and...
this song could be you, could be...
that with-out you there's no point
E
A
B
3.
E
This to this song.
This
Repeat and fade
E
Repeat and fade

TRUE LOVE

from HIGH SOCIETY

Words and Music by
COLE PORTER

D
A
Em7
ways be
true
love,
true
A7
D
Gm7
3 fr.
C7
love.
For you
and
I
have
a guard-
F
Dm
Gm7
3 fr.
ian
an
-
gel
on
high
with
noth-
C7
F
A7
ing
to
do
but
to
give

D
G
D°7
D
to me and to give to you
Em7
A7
Bm7
a love for - ev - er true;
D
Em7
A7
it's a love for - ev - er true.
B♭7
D°7
D

UNCONSCIOUSNESS RULES

Words and Music by
GEORGE HARRISON

E7

You've got that look in your eyes __ that says __ you're half __
You've got a way and a stance __ that says __ you'll dance __
You lost a screw in your head. __ It shows __ the way __

D

__ a - live __ and you're lost __ in - side. __
__ the pants __ off of ev - 'ry - one. __
__ you're led, __ blind lead - ing __ the blind. __

Tacet

A7 E7

Mean-while you're back in your cage, __ e - go'd out on the stage __
Then you go back on the floor. __ You got to get through the door __
Noth - ing can stand in your way. __ You're liv - ing day af - ter day __

A7 D A7

Tacet

where the un-con-scious-ness rules. Do do do do do do

E7 A7 D

do do do do do do do do do do do.

1. *Tacet* A7 2. *Tacet* A7 3. *Tacet* A7

You've got your-self in a bind. Oh yeah,

E7 A7 D

oh yeah, un-con-scious-ness rules.

WHEN WE WAS FAB

Words and Music by JEFF LYNNE
and GEORGE HARRISON

B♭7
(Fab! Doot, doot, doot, doo.) Long time a go __ when we was
C
fab.
B♭7
(Fab.)
F
Back when in - come tax was all
C
we had,
F
G
Am
Ca - ress - ers fleeced you in the morn-
The mi - cro- scopes that mag - ni - fied _

F7
Am
- ing light,
ca - sual - ties at dawn.
the tears
stud - ied warts and
B7
all.
And we did it all.
Still the life flowed on
C/E
Am6
Fm/A♭
B♭7
and on.
(Fab! Doot, doot, doot,
C
doo.) Long time a - go when we was fab.
(Gear!)

B♭7
F
(Fab.)
You're my world you are my on - ly love.
But it's all o - ver now, ba - by blue.
C
To Coda
F/A
Dm7
And while you're in this world
G
F/C
Dm7
G7
C
the fuzz gon-na come and claim you.
F/A
Dm7
G
F/C
Dm7
But you mo bet - ter wise
when the buzz gon-na come and take

G
C
F#o
you a - way.
Take you a - way.
Fm6
C/E
F#o
F6
Fm6
C
Take you a - way.
D.S. al Coda
CODA

B♭
(Oo! Doot, doot, doot. Fab!) Long time a - go when we was
C
B♭7
F
fab. (Fab!) Like this pull - o - ver you sent
C
B♭7
to me. (Fab! Doot, doot, doot.
C
B♭7
Gear!)

F
C
And you real - ly got a hold on me.
B♭7
(Fab! Doot, doot, doot. Gear!) Long time a - go __ when we was
C
B♭7
F
fab.
C

UNKNOWN DELIGHT

Words and Music by
GEORGE HARRISON

Bm
Bm7
An - gel came in - to my dream.
God has giv - en you the key
And no one could dis - a - gree.
E7♭9/G♯
3fr
A
Like the morn - ing's ear - ly light,
to the hearts of ev - 'ry - one
A treas - ure of the world.
F♯(add2)
F♯
Bm
you fresh - en all a - round.
that comes in sight of you.
A child watch - ing it grow.
G7
A
Amaj7
A7
A6
And with all the love you bring un - known de - light.
And with all the love you bring un - known de - light.
And with all the love will bring un - known de - light.

Dm
A
Amaj7
A7
Umm, you bring
All the love you bring
All the love will bring
A6
Dm
To Coda
A
un - known de - light.
un - known de - light.
un - known de - light.
A
Amaj7
A7
Bm

Bm7 E7♭9/G♯ 3fr

A F♯(add2) F♯ Bm

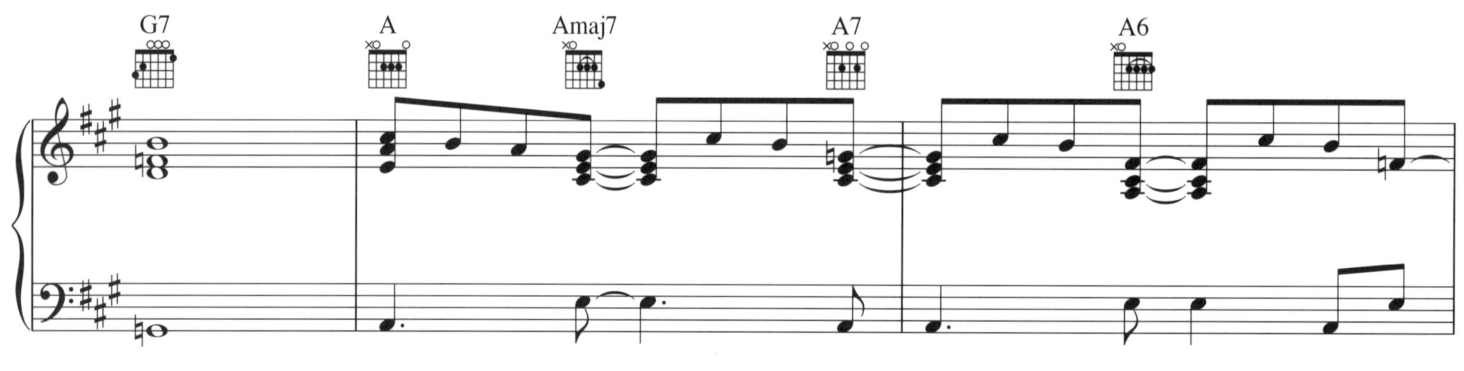

A6
Dm
A
un - known de - light.
D.S. al Coda
CODA
A
Amaj7
A7
A6
Dm
Un - known de - light.
A
Amaj7
A7
A6
All the love will bring un - known de - light.

Dm
A
Amaj7
A7
(Lead vocal ad lib. on repeat)
A6
Dm
A
Amaj7
A7
A6
All the love will bring un - known de - light.
Dm
A
Repeat and Fade
Optional Ending

WAKE UP MY LOVE

Words and Music by
GEORGE HARRISON

G
D
C
D
me in? Only want that same old thing.
that clear. All I've had's the run-around
me crazed. All around us people fight.
that pipe. Not much sense in what they do.
G
D
G
C
This is me here, ring ring ring. I want Your love.
though I'm barking like some hound. Don't want Your love.
Christ, I'm looking for some light inside Your love.
That is why I'm calling You inside my love.
Am7
Wake up my love and let it in.
C/D
G
1,3

2,4
Am7
C/D
To Coda
I want Your love.
Wake up my love
and let it
G
D
C/D
D
in.
G/D
D
G/D
C
G
D
C
D
G
D
G
C

1
2
Am7
C/D
G
D.S. al Coda
CODA
G
in.
Wake up my
Am7
C/D
G
love. Wake up my love and let it in.

D C D
Oh, I need
I get tired of wrong
G D G C
it, Lord.
and right.
Oh, I need
You can see I need
G D C D
You more.
Your light.
There's this emp - ti - ness
And that's me knock -
G D G C
out - side.
- ing on Your door
You know, Lord it's ris -
and it's You I'm look -

G
D
C
D
- ing wide.
- ing for.
Oh Lord.
G
D
G
C
Oh Lord.
Am7
C/D
Wake up my love and let it in.
G
Am7
Repeat and Fade
I want to love. Wake up my

WOMAN DON'T YOU CRY FOR ME

Words and Music by
GEORGE HARRISON

E
I'm gon-na leave you at the sta - tion.
I've got a long way to go, ba-by. Wom-an, don't you cry for me.
Now I can't take no more;
I don't need no com-pli-ca - tion.

I've got a long way to go, ba - by. Wom - an, don't you
cry for me.
There's
There's
A
no one place I want_ to be; at - tach - ment on - ly hurts_ me.
no one place I want_ to be; at - tach - ment on - ly hurts_ you.
B
G
E
Take care of your - self, ba - by; c'- mon, won't you let me be.
Take care of your - self, ba - by; c'- mon, won't you try to see.

A
There's_ just one thing I got_ to see:_that's the
There's_ just one thing I got_ to see:_that's the
B
E/D
Lord; got to keep him in sight. Take care of your-self, ba-by; c'-mon, won't you let me be._
Lord; got to keep him in sight. Bet-ter take care of your-self, ba-by; c'-mon, won't you let me be._
E
1.
Instrumental
2.
Now, ba - by, here's the_ door;_

E
I don't need no ag-gra-va - tion.
I've got a long way to go, ba - by. Wom - an, don't you cry for me.
I'm gon - na leave you here,
I'm gon - na leave you at the sta - tion.

I've got a long way to go, ba - by. Wom - an, don't you
cry for me.
I've got a long way to
go, ba - by. Wom - an, don't you cry for me.
f

WRECK OF THE HESPERUS

Words and Music by
GEORGE HARRISON

Em Em/D A7 B7

Get-ting old as Me-thu - s'lah. Feel tall as the Eif-
Ain't no more no spring chick - en. Been plucked, but I'm

Em Em/D B♭dim7 G7

- fel Tow - er.
still kick - in'.
(2nd time only:) (But it's al - right, it's

B♭dim7 G7 | 1 C/G G7 N.C. | 2 Bm/F♯

al - right.)

Em C7 Am7

Poi-son pen - men sneak, have no nerve to speak; make up lies, they leak

Em
C7
'em out.
Be-hind a pseu-do-nym,
the rot-ten-ness in them
Am7
B7
G7
reach-ing out, try'n' to touch me.
Met some Os-cars and To-
C7
G7
C
B7/D♯
nys.
I slipped on a pave-ment oy-ster.
Em
Em/D
A7
B7
Met a snake climb-ing lad-ders.
Got out of the line

Em
Em/D
B♭dim7
G7
of fire.
(Well it's al - right.)
B♭dim7
G7
B♭dim7
G7
B♭dim7
G7
Bm/F♯
Em
Brain - less writ - ers
C7
Am7
Em
gos - sip non - sens - es to oth - er heads dense as they is. It's

C7
Am7
the same old mal - a - dy;
what they see is
B7
G7
C7
faul - ty.
I'm not the wreck of the Hes - p'rus.
G7
C
B7/D♯
Em
Em/D
Feel more like Big Bill Broon - zy.
Get-tin' old as my moth-
A7
B7
Em
Em/D
- er;
but I tell you, I got some com - pa - ny.
(Well it's al -

B♭dim7 G7 B♭dim7 G7

right.)

C/G G7 N.C.

B♭dim7 G7

(Vocals tacet first time)

right,

Instrumental solo

B♭dim7 G7

Repeat and Fade

it's al - right.) (Well it's al -

Optional Ending

C/G G7 N.C.

WRITINGS ON THE WALL

Words and Music by
GEORGE HARRISON

D G

wall. It looks you in the eye,
wall. The mu-sic's in the air,
grow. The writ-ing's on the wall,

D Em7-5 Gm/A 3fr. D

mis-ter. It's time we stand up tall.
moth-ers. You may have heard it call
broth-ers. Your life is in your hands.

G#o7 D E7 A7sus4 *To Coda*

Go see and un-der-stand the writ-ing's on the
to you that you may see the writ-ing's on the
It's up to you to see the writ-ing's on the

D
wall.
wall.
D
Gm/D
Strange, we hold on to things that have
Vocal tacet
D
Gm/D
D
no grace or power while death holds on to us
Gm/D
D
B♭
much more with ev - 'ry pass - ing hour.
And

A7
D
Bm
all the time you thought it would last; your
A7
D
B♭7
life, your friends would always be.
Em7
A7
Em7
A7
Till they're drunk a-way or shot a-way or
Em7
A7
D
1.
die a-way from you.

2.
D.S. 𝄋 al Coda
Coda
D
wall.
G♯o7
D
I hope that you may see the writ - ing's
E7
A7sus4
D
G♯o7
on the wall.
D
E7
A7sus4
D
poco rit.

YOUR LOVE IS FOREVER

Words and Music by
GEORGE HARRISON

D
like heav-en's a - bout here.
flames burn-ing, I know.
Gmaj7
G6
Asus4
A
Dmaj7
But un-like sum-mer came and went, your love is for - ev -
But un-like win - ter came and went, your love is for - ev -
D
Asus4
er. I feel it, and my heart knows that
er. I feel it, and my heart knows that
A
Asus4
C/G
G
A
To Coda
D.S. al Coda
we share it to - geth - er.
we share it to -

Coda
G
A
D
Asus4
geth - er. I feel it, and my heart knows you're
F
Csus4
the one. The guid - ing light in all your love
C
D
Asus4
shines on. The on - ly lov - er worth it all.
A
Asus4
C/G
G
D
Your love is for - ev - er.
rit.

ZIG ZAG

Words and Music by GEORGE HARRISON
and JEFF LYNNE

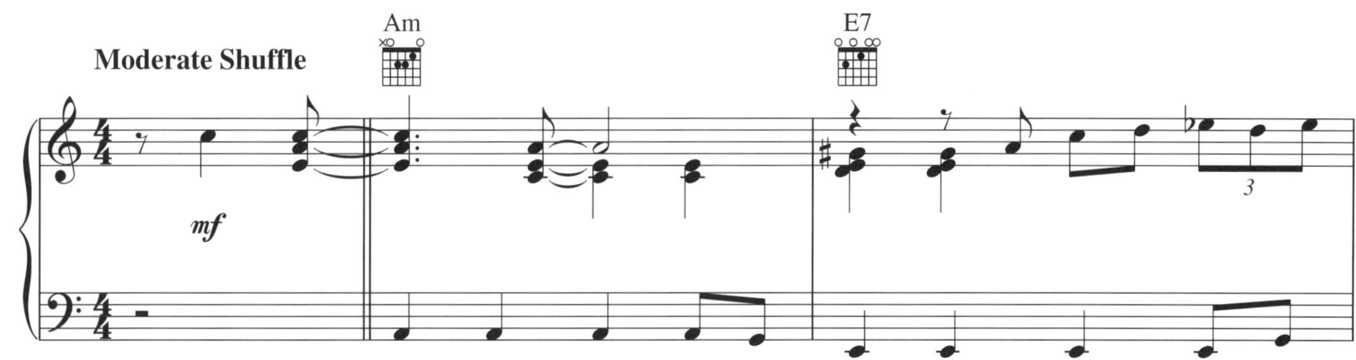

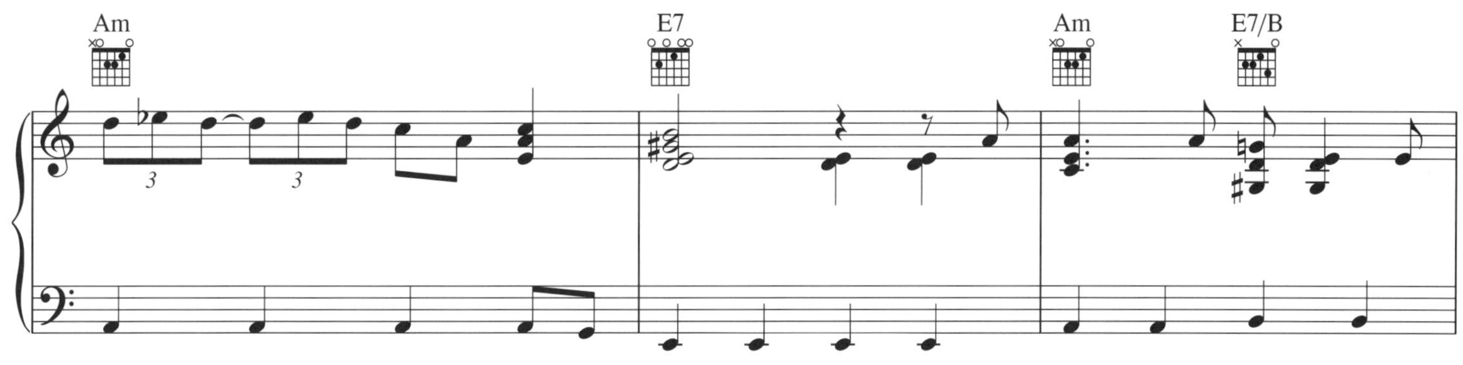

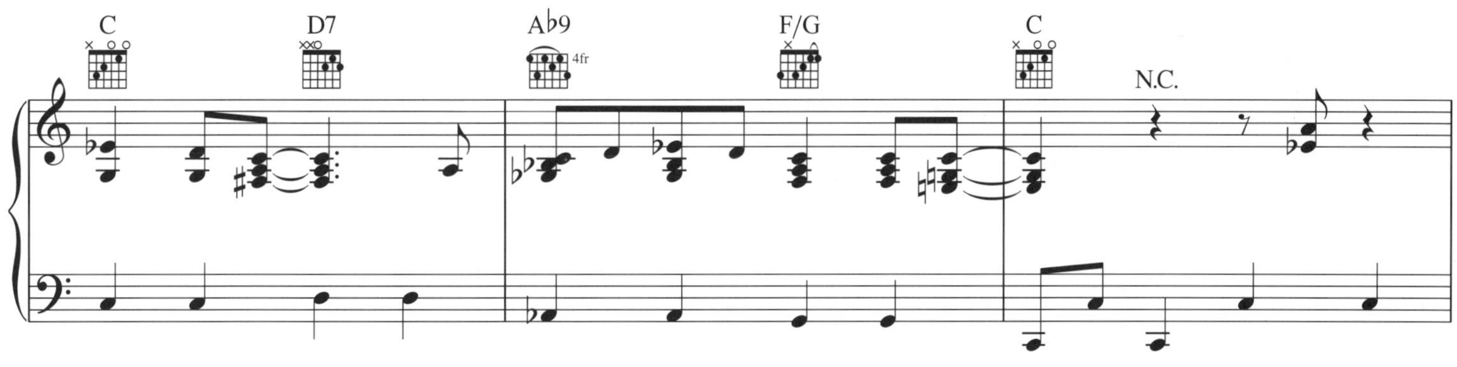

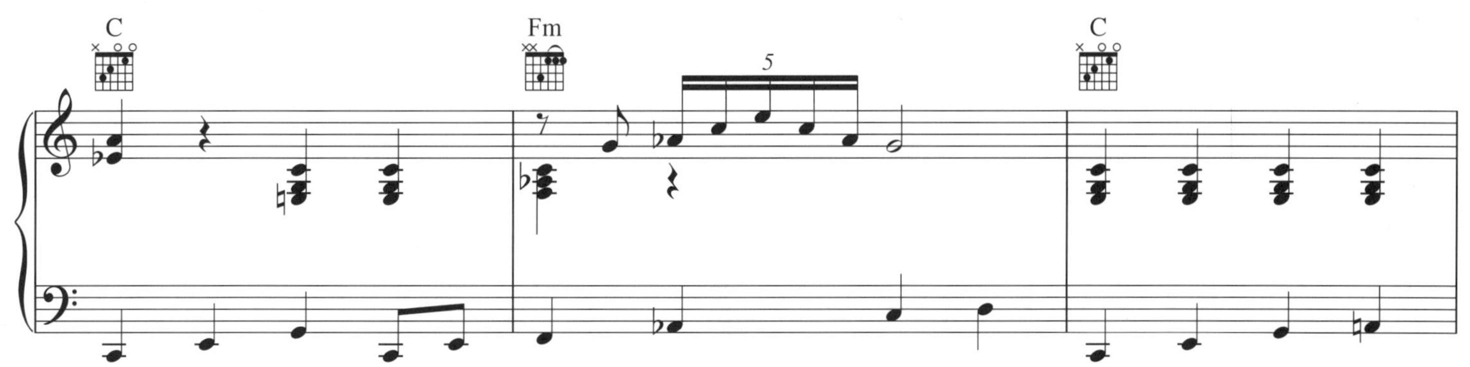

Fm
C
Am
5
Fm
A♭9
4fr
G7♯5
C
Fm
Zig
zag.
Zig
C
Fm
C
Am
zag.
Zig
zag.
Fm
A♭9
4fr
G9
9fr
Am
E7
Doot doot doot.
Doot doot doot.
Instrumental solo

Am
E7
Am
E7/B
Doot doot doot.
Doot doot doot.
C
D7
A♭9
4fr
F/G
Am
D9
4fr
A♭9
4fr
G9
9fr
C
N.C.
C
Fm
Oh, zig zag.
C
Fm
C
Am

Fm
A♭9
4fr
G7♯5
C
Fm
Zig
zag.
Zig
Solo ends.
3
C
Fm
C
Am
zag.
Zig
zag.
3
Fm
1 A♭7
4fr
G7
2 A♭7
4fr
G7
Am
E7/B
C
D7
A♭9
4fr
G9
9fr
C
N.C.
Oh, ______
zig
zag.